Third World Debt: The Next Phase

Edited by EDWARD R. FRIED
PHILIP H. TREZISE

Report of a conference held in Washington, D.C., on

March 10, 1989, sponsored by the Bretton Woods Committee

and the Brookings Institution, chaired by Charls E. Walker

THE BROOKINGS INSTITUTION / Washington, D.C.

Copyright © 1989 by

THE BROOKINGS INSTITUTION

1775 Massachusetts Avenue, N.W.

Washington, D.C. 20036

LIBRARY OF CONGRESS CATALOG CARD NUMBER 89-062015

ISBN 0-8157-2977-4

9 8 7 6 5 4 3 2 1

About Brookings

The Brookings Institution is a private nonprofit organization devoted to research, education, and publication in economics, government, foreign policy, and the social sciences generally. Its principal purpose is to bring knowledge to bear on the current and emerging public policy problems facing the American people. In its research, Brookings functions as an independent analyst and critic, committed to publishing its findings for the information of the public. In its conferences and other activities, it serves as a bridge between scholarship and public policy, bringing new knowledge to the attention of decisionmakers and affording scholars a better insight into policy issues. Its activities are carried out through three research programs (Economic Studies, Governmental Studies, Foreign Policy Studies), a Center for Public Policy Education, a Publications Program, and a Social Science Computation Center.

The Institution was incorporated in 1927 to merge the Institute for Government Research, founded in 1916 as the first private organization devoted to public policy issues at the national level; the Institute of Economics, established in 1922 to study economic problems; and the Robert Brookings Graduate School of Economics and Government, organized in 1924 as a pioneering experiment in training for public service. The consolidated institution was named in honor of Robert Somers Brookings (1850–1932), a St. Louis businessman whose leadership shaped the earlier organizations.

Brookings is financed largely by endowment and by the support of philanthropic foundations, corporations, and private individuals. Its funds are devoted to carrying out its own research and educational activities. It also undertakes some unclassified government contract studies, reserving the right to publish its findings.

A Board of Trustees is responsible for general supervision of the Institution, approval of fields of investigation, and safeguarding the independence of the Institution's work. The President is the chief administrative officer, responsible for formulating and coordinating policies, recommending projects, approving publications, and selecting staff.

Board of Trustees

Louis W. Cabot
Chairman

Ralph S. Saul
Vice Chairman

Ronald Arnault
Elizabeth E. Bailey
Rex J. Bates
Yvonne B. Burke
A. W. Clausen

William T. Coleman, Jr.
Kenneth W. Dam
D. Ronald Daniel
Richard G. Darman
Charles W. Duncan, Jr.
Walter Y. Elisha
Robert F. Erburu
Robert D. Haas
Pamela C. Harriman
Vernon E. Jordan, Jr.
James A. Joseph
Thomas G. Labrecque

Donald F. McHenry
Bruce K. MacLaury
Mary Patterson McPherson
Donald S. Perkins
James D. Robinson III
Howard D. Samuel
B. Francis Saul II
Henry B. Schacht
Howard R. Swearer
Morris Tanenbaum
James D. Wolfensohn
Ezra K. Zilkha

Honorary Trustees

Vincent M. Barnett, Jr.
Barton M. Biggs
Eugene R. Black
Robert D. Calkins
Edward W. Carter
Frank T. Cary
Lloyd N. Cutler
Bruce B. Dayton
Douglas Dillon

Huntington Harris
Andrew Heiskell
Roger W. Heyns
Roy M. Huffington
John E. Lockwood
James T. Lynn
William McC. Martin, Jr.
Robert S. McNamara
Arjay Miller

J. Woodward Redmond
Charles W. Robinson
Robert V. Roosa
H. Chapman Rose
Gerard C. Smith
Robert Brookings Smith
Sydney Stein, Jr.
Phyllis A. Wallace
Charles J. Zwick

Editors' Preface

Third world debt appeared on the global economic scene as a crisis in August 1982, when the government of Mexico announced that it could no longer meet current obligations to its foreign creditors. Since 1982 the crisis has declined to the status of a chronic problem, but a problem that continues to present serious economic and political dangers for debtor and creditor countries alike.

The new U.S. administration has now moved beyond past policy by proposing official financial support for debt reduction, that is, for negotiated and market-based transactions to reduce the cost of servicing the external debt of those countries undertaking or prepared to undertake domestic economic policy reforms. This reflects a recognition that earlier assumptions about the willingness of commercial bank creditors to continue lending have proved ill founded, and a concern that the size of the debt overhang is itself a barrier to economic recovery. It also responds to the evidence of a worrisome deterioration of the political situation in some of the most important debtor countries.

Whether the planned use of relatively modest World Bank and International Monetary Fund monies, supplemented by Japan's Export-Import Bank lending, will sufficiently ease debtors' burdens remains to be seen. In any event, a new phase in the international approach to third world debt has been opened. Its unfolding will have repercussions, for better or worse, for welfare everywhere.

To address the issues involved in debt reduction and the debt overhang, the Bretton Woods Committee and the Brookings Institution cosponsored a conference held at the U.S. Department of State on March 10, 1989. At the conference, Secretary of the Treasury Nicholas Brady made public the essence of and the arguments for the change in official policy. This volume includes his speech along with statements and commentary by heads of the principal international financial institutions, members of the U.S. Congress, commercial bank leaders, and other financial experts. Charls E. Walker was chairman of the conference. Paul A. Volcker was chairman and interlocutor of the panel on Status, Issues, and Prospects. Henry D. Owen was chairman and interlocutor of the panel on Perspectives of Commercial Bank Creditors. Bruce K. MacLaury was chairman and interlocutor of the panels on Perspectives of Politicians and Concluding Impressions. Caroline Lalire edited the manuscript; Janet E. Smith and Susan L. Woollen prepared it for typesetting.

The editors are grateful to the Sloan Foundation, the American Express Company, and the Kidder Peabody Group for helping to finance the conference and to the Ford Foundation for helping to finance the publication.

The views expressed in this volume are those of the authors, commentators, and participants and should not be ascribed to the sponsoring institutions or to their trustees, officers, or other staff members.

July 1988   Edward R. Fried
Washington, D.C.   Philip H. Trezise

Contents

Overview

Edward R. Fried and Philip H. Trezise

This volume is the record of a conference held on March 10, 1989, that, in the event, centered on a departure from the basic U.S. policy toward the long-standing problem of third world debt. Secretary of the Treasury Nicholas Brady took the occasion of the conference to announce that officially sponsored reduction of debt principal and debt interest should henceforth be an integral part of debt strategy. Promptly labeled the Brady plan, the secretary's statement has since been the subject of extensive debate at home and abroad. Now that it has been given official sanction, debt service reduction has become an inescapable feature of the ongoing effort to manage and resolve the debt problem.

We propose in this essay to consider the implications of introducing debt and debt service reduction into the preexisting menu of policies and, more specifically, to suggest the conditions under which it can be expected to hasten the removal of the third world debt problem from the international economic agenda. In doing so, we hope to reflect both the discussion at the conference and the subsequent debate and surrounding events.

REASONS FOR THE SHIFT IN U.S. POLICY

A starting point can be put as a question. After having long and resolutely resisted proposals for writing down the amount of debt or for easing the terms of outstanding loans, why did the U.S. administration change course this year? The answer seems most likely to be found in two developments that by early 1989 had become especially damaging to ongoing policy or to complacency about the debt situation.

One was evidence that the net flow of funds from private banks to the heavily indebted middle-income countries had turned negative, even significantly so. Under Secretary James A. Baker's initiative of

1985, private banks had been counted on to supply some $7 billion a year in "new" money—that is, net disbursements minus repayments of principal—to these countries. That amount would have financed roughly one-third of the interest due to private banks on their outstanding loans to these countries, since 1985 known as the Baker 15.[1]

In reality, net commercial bank lending to these countries amounted to only $1 billion in 1986, $1 billion in 1987, and a negative $4 billion in 1988. Thus the largest single source of projected capital flows to support economic recovery in these countries had failed to come even remotely close to the target. Furthermore, such new lending as had taken place in 1987–88 was concentrated on concerted new lending packages for Argentina, Brazil, and Mexico. Some smaller debtors that had succeeded in putting promising economic policy measures into effect—notably Chile, Morocco, and the Philippines— were unable to get new commercial bank credit. The banks' evident concentration on reducing their exposure suggested that a return to voluntary lending to third world countries on a large scale was much further off than had been contemplated. Debt service reduction of some kind then became a necessary alternative, in part or in whole, to new lending.

The other disturbing development that called for a reexamination of debt strategy was the changing political situation in Latin America. In March 1989 the new Carlos Andrés Pérez administration in Venezuela faced riots when it reduced government subsidies as part of an economic policy reform package negotiated with the International Monetary Fund. Similarly, the Carlos Salinas de Gortari administration in Mexico, which has gone furthest in restructuring economic policy, clearly needs additional external help to continue its reform program in the face of a tenuous internal political position. Later in this book William Rogers gives a graphic description of the current political unrest in Latin America generally, stemming from poor economic performance and a reduction in living standards in the 1980s.

Rightly or wrongly, heavy debt service burdens are considered to

1. Secretary Baker's list consists of Argentina, Bolivia, Brazil, Chile, Colombia, Ecuador, the Ivory Coast, Mexico, Morocco, Nigeria, Peru, the Philippines, Uruguay, Venezuela, and Yugoslavia. In its category of heavily indebted countries, the World Bank adds Costa Rica and Jamaica.

be largely responsible for these results and a barrier to economic recovery. Thus the debt problem had become a potentially destabilizing political force in the region, a fact made the more worrisome because, as was pointed out in the conference discussion, twelve presidential elections are scheduled in Latin America over an eighteen-month period. One, in Argentina, has since been held; as expected, the winner was Carlos Menem, leader of the populist Peronist party. In these circumstances, negotiated debt reduction, apart from its economic value, could be useful political ammunition for leaders engaged in ongoing economic policy reform.

A BREAKDOWN OF THE THIRD WORLD DEBT

Before examining the Brady initiative, it is useful to review the specifics of third world debt. The total now seems to have stabilized at $1.3 trillion, about 50 percent of GNP. Adjusted for inflation, it is about 25 percent larger than it was in 1982.

That is a large number, to be sure, but a breakdown helps us to understand the kind of problem it poses.

—Some 12 percent is short-term trade finance, which normally is rolled over without much difficulty.

—Another 5 percent is owed by low-income sub-Saharan African countries, which are dependent on concessional capital from industrial country governments and the multilateral financial agencies. Governments belonging to the Organization for Economic Cooperation and Development (OECD) are rescheduling or writing off these loans, or reducing interest rates on them, to encourage policy reform and recovery programs. Private banks are not a factor here.

—Roughly 45 percent of outstanding long-term debt is owed by some fifty countries, whose debt, on the whole, seems manageable. There are trouble spots and reschedulings in this group, but interest payments average a reasonable 7 percent of exports of goods and services. OECD governments are either the creditors or guarantors of 60 percent of this debt; private banks are at risk for 40 percent and continue to be voluntary suppliers of new money to some of these countries.

—The highly indebted countries account for the remaining 38 percent, or $480 billion in medium- and long-term debt. For most purposes they constitute the third world debt problem and are the subject of the Brady initiative, as they were of predecessor programs. Private banks hold 64 percent of this debt, the multilateral banks 19 percent, and OECD governments 17 percent. Four-fifths is concentrated in Latin America, heavily so in Brazil, Mexico, Argentina, and Venezuela. Economic and debt difficulties in this group are severe. In 1988 interest obligations averaged 25 percent of exports of goods and services and 4 percent of GNP. Investment is still depressed: 15 percent of GNP in 1988 compared with 25 percent in 1980. A large net outflow of resources continues, and economic growth in 1987–88 was under 2 percent, less than population growth. In 1988 per capita consumption for the group as a whole was 5 percent below what it was at the beginning of the decade.

THE OPERATION OF THE BRADY PLAN

How does the Brady plan propose to deal with this rather bleak picture?

Sensibly, and inevitably, the new strategy builds on rather than replaces the essential features of the Baker plan, a necessity widely supported by speakers at the conference. It recognizes that a favorable resolution of the debt problem requires higher economic growth, which in turn depends on economic policy reforms designed to use resources more efficiently, encourage domestic savings and investment, and attract capital from abroad, including the repatriation of flight capital. The World Bank and the IMF, supported by the regional development banks, continue to be seen as having the central responsibility for promoting structural improvements in the debtor countries. As before, the approach is case by case rather than comprehensive, with external financing, from these institutions, private banks, and governments, tied to policy performance.

The Brady initiative represents change mainly in offering for the first time official financial support for negotiated debt and debt service reductions. Voluntary or market-based debt reduction had already been part of the menu approach under the Baker plan. Indeed, in 1988 the highly indebted countries, principally Mexico, Brazil, and Chile, had extinguished, at a discount, approximately $15 billion in commercial bank debt (an increase from $8 billion in 1987) through debt-for-equity swaps, debt-for-debt exchanges, and debt buybacks. Now the objective is to increase the volume of these transactions.

Under the Brady plan the World Bank and the IMF would make loans earmarked to enable debtor governments to negotiate debt reduction transactions with the commercial banks. With these funds available as collateral, the debtors could offer to exchange their debt to commercial banks at a discount for new bonds or at par for bonds carrying reduced rates of interest, or combinations of both. Or they could use the funds to buy back their bank debt at a discount for cash. In a significant departure from earlier practice, the debtor governments could be given assurance of World Bank and IMF lending before they reached agreement on what the commercial banks would do, a step that would give them needed help more expeditiously and could also strengthen their bargaining position with the commercial banks.

Soon after the Brady speech the U.S. initiative received the general endorsement of the Group of 7 (the major industrialized nations), the IMF Interim Committee, and the World Bank's Development Committee. West Germany and Great Britain expressed reservations about the implied increase in OECD government responsibility for commercial bank debt but did not reject the proposal.

Operational guidelines subsequently worked out by the World Bank and the IMF indicate that $20–$25 billion will be available over three years to support debt reduction through so-called credit enhancements, roughly half from each institution. Of this total, $11 billion could be used to support negotiated reductions in interest payments. These funds would be additional to loans that the two institutions would otherwise be prepared to extend. The remainder, approximately half the total, could be used to support negotiated reductions of debt principal. This latter portion falls within ongoing lending guidelines and in this sense would probably not be additional. Terms of individual transactions negotiated by the debtor countries with the commercial banks will be subject to the approval of the lending institutions—that is, the World Bank and the IMF—which should add to the negotiating leverage of the country and help to ensure that the transactions are an efficient use of scarce financial resources.

Official lending for debt reduction is limited to debt-distressed countries committed to structural adjustment and policy reform, a proviso that will tend to limit the number of eligible debtor countries. At the same time, the commercial banks are asked to provide temporary general waivers to the sharing and negative pledge clauses in existing loan agreements for performing countries so as to facilitate quick negotiation of debt reduction operations.[2] They are also counted on to continue lending for trade finance and project loans and to continue to participate in concerted new lending packages. For their part, debtor countries are expected to maintain viable debt-equity swap programs as an additional means of reducing debt service burdens and promoting investment.

In support of this new approach, Japan announced it would commit $4.5 billion over the next three years for additional lending by its Export-Import Bank in parallel with IMF lending to the highly indebted countries. Indications are that Japan will commit an additional amount for lending in parallel with World Bank programs. In recent years Japan's Ex-Im Bank lending has moved somewhat beyond export finance. Pending legislation, described in Seigo Nozaki's presentation, would broaden its authorities further. The mandate of that Bank, however, essentially confines it to lending at commercial or near-commercial terms to credible borrowers. It can be expected to disburse its added resources with some caution.

POTENTIAL IMPACT

How will this debt reduction initiative fit in with the ongoing effort to promote an orderly debt resolution, or more important to promote the stronger economic growth on which an orderly debt resolution ultimately depends? Michel Camdessus, managing director of the IMF, reported staff projections to the effect that continued adjustment efforts in debtor countries and a reasonably favorable external environment could permit a moderate economic recovery in debtor countries to 4 percent a year, or double the 1988 level, over the next three to five years.

2. These clauses are individually specified in loan agreements. Generally, negative pledges obligate borrowers *not* to pledge assets or future earnings to one creditor to the prejudice of other creditors. Sharing clauses require borrowers, when meeting payment obligations, to share assets and earnings proportionately among all participating creditors. A borrowing country may have several hundred bank creditors with differing interests and preferences about the form of debt reduction and the size of the discount. Therefore, obtaining individual waivers of these claims in order to complete a debt reduction transaction could be a difficult and prolonged process.

More specifically, World Bank studies have emphasized that restoring growth in the highly indebted countries to the 4–5 percent level over the next several years would require continued improvements in the internal efficiency of resource use, together with an inflow of some $20 billion a year in medium- and long-term capital from all sources: direct foreign investment, bilateral governmental aid and credits, loans from multilateral development banks and the IMF, and new lending from private commercial banks. Short-term trade finance would be additional. This strong link between internal policy improvement and capital inflows was stressed throughout the conference, as it is in the World Bank's analysis. Indeed, Enrique Iglesias, president of the Inter-American Development Bank, argued that the winds of economic reform were blowing strongly in Latin America but said they could only be exploited fully if the negative transfer of resources from the region was significantly reduced.

Of the $20 billion in capital inflows projected as needed by the World Bank, the critical portion is the $7 billion or so attributed to new commercial bank loans. With good policy performance, the other $13 billion seems attainable. From recent experience, however, new lending on this order by the commercial banks seems to be out of the question. Nor can the shortfall be made up elsewhere. For the international financial institutions to seek to do so would quickly overwhelm their lending capacity, if not their credit standing. Furthermore, such a shift in debt liabilities from private to public sources would be difficult to justify and would not get the approval of OECD governments; as Congressman Jim Leach put it, "capitalists should be held accountable for capitalist mistakes."

This was the dilemma the Brady initiative sought to address. New medium- and long-term bank lending of $7 billion a year, no longer in prospect, would represent about one-third the interest payments due the banks on their outstanding loans to the highly indebted countries. It follows, therefore, that a negotiated reduction of one-third in debt principal or interest rates would have the same effect as $7 billion a year in new lending, with the added political bonus that debt reduction could provide to hard-pressed debtor country administrations.

Measured against this standard, the $20–$25 billion available to support debt reduction under the Brady initiative is much too small. For example, if the total amount, say $25 billion, were used to guarantee new bonds issued in exchange for bank debt at a discount of 50 percent, the total bank debt would be reduced by $50 billion, or about 15 percent. Total debt, however, would be reduced by only half this amount, since the additional debt owed to the IMF and the World Bank would replace half the commercial bank debt that had been retired. The same result would apply to interest payments if the same funds were used entirely to guarantee principal and interest on bonds having the same par value as existing debt but issued at interest rates 50 percent lower than prevailing bank rates. Either way, the potential savings in debt-servicing payments would amount to $2.5 billion a year (that is, assuming an interest rate of 10 percent on a net retirement of $25 billion in debt). That would be equal to about one-third the new lending needed from the banks. Even this result, moreover, would be attained only over several years. These results apply to the category of highly indebted countries as a whole, only some of which are close to meeting policy performance requirements. Thus proportionately larger amounts could be allocated for debt and interest rate reduction transactions to Mexico, the Philippines, Costa Rica, and Venezuela to begin with, but the general financial limitations on the program would still apply.

The gap of course could be filled by a combination of debt reduction and new lending. At the outset of the conference Paul Volcker pointedly remarked on "the simple arithmetic" that in terms of immediate cash flow a given amount of new money is equal to ten times that amount of debt reduction, since the first-year contribution of the latter is limited to savings on interest at the assumed rate of 10 percent. If debt reduction alone cannot meet financing needs, as he thought likely, then the problem of how to sustain an adequate flow of new money remains, possibly under worsened circumstances. Former Mexican finance minister Jesús Silva Herzog argued that it was indeed necessary to reduce debt and sustain a flow of fresh money. He was confident that ways could be found to accomplish both despite the apparent incompatibility between them. Others were not so sure, particularly in view of the weighted average discount of 60 percent on secondary market prices for outstanding bank loans to the highly indebted countries. In other words, new loans put on the books at par would have a market value of only 40 percent of par. Secretary Brady seemed to be addressing this problem when he noted in his speech that "consideration could be given in some cases to ways of differentiating new from old debt."

Repatriation of flight capital is another possible source of funds. The potential is very large; capital amounting to as much as 50 percent of outstanding debt may have moved abroad during this decade. But as Barber Conable, president of the World Bank, noted, capital cannot be ordered back; it moves toward favorable economic environments and away from unfavorable economic environments. Once policy improvements are put into place and recovery is under way, flight capital is likely to be repatriated. Thus it could be a large, cumulative positive factor in the medium term. In the short term, however, some front-loading of other capital inflows will be needed; otherwise net outflows of resources could stymie the recovery process that is needed to bring flight capital home.

This raises the question of how to get the optimum up-front reduction in debt service payments from the funds used to support debt relief under the Brady initiative so as to get the recovery process off to a solid start. Given the limited amounts that are to be available from the IMF and the World Bank, leveraging their use over the next several years becomes a critical variable. An obvious possibility would be to keep the period covered by guarantees as brief as possible in debt relief packages, while still providing demonstrable benefits to debtors and creditors alike.

Suppose, for example, that twenty-year bonds used to replace a debtor nation's existing bank debt would carry an interest rate at 50 percent of the original rate for the first five years, with an explicit understanding that after year 5 the rate would be negotiated in the light of the country's progress toward creditworthiness or, in some cases, the course of world prices for its principal export commodities. IMF or World Bank funds committed to guaranteeing payment of the lowered rate for short periods would go much further than if the guarantee provision were extended to the maturity of the bond. Thus the Brady initiative's potential for debt relief in the short term would be the larger—and the need for new commercial bank lending the smaller. In these circumstances, moreover, the creditor banks could defer the issue of a write-off of debt principal. Meanwhile their interest income during the initial period would be reduced but also ensured and the risk of added arrearages avoided. The interest rate proposals in Tom Clausen's statement seem to be in this direction.

Similar considerations apply to guarantees of reduced debt principal. The shorter the time during which guarantees are to be effective, the greater the up-front leverage to be gained from the application of the Brady approach. It is important to recognize that maximum relief for eligible debtors over the next few years may well be the most critical requirement. To be sure, the necessary debtor-creditor negotiations would take place under a known constraint, but there would be gains for both in sight.

MEXICO AS THE TEST CASE

From the beginning, Mexico has been seen as the test case of the new strategy. At the conference Conable called Mexico "a good place to start. It has demonstrated a willingness to undertake major reforms and has lived up to its obligations. Mexico's debt is very large, but so is its potential. In return for maintaining and deepening the economic policy changes and the structural adjustments Mexico has put in place in the past five years, the international financial community should help to give Mexico a wider than usual range of options to finance external capital requirements over the next several years." He emphasized that debt reduction, strong lending programs by the multilateral institutions, and new money from the commercial banks would be necessary. It is also worth noting that Mexico alone accounts for one-fourth of the medium- and long-term debt of the Baker 15 and clearly has the economic potential to grow out of its debt problem. Reducing Mexico's debt overhang and interest payments to manageable proportions in the near term, coupled with a significant flow of new lending, would demonstrate that the Brady strategy could be effective.

Mexico is seeking to reduce its net transfers abroad from 6 percent to 2 percent of GNP as a necessary step in its program to push economic recovery to 4 percent in 1990. The IMF, the World Bank, the Inter-American Bank, and Japan have put together a package of $6 billion over three years in lending for Mexico, principally to support debt and interest rate reduction. Most critically, Mexico has asked for $4.5 billion a year from its commercial banks, to be obtained from a combination of debt service reduction and new lending. On debt reduction, Mexico seeks discounts of 55 percent, near the discount prevailing for its debt in secondary markets. So far, the commercial banks have offered less than half this amount and are being pressed by the U.S. Treasury and the IMF managing director to do much more.

ARE THERE ALTERNATIVES?

Hard bargaining understandably lies ahead for Mexico and for other performing countries where the international institutions have already made, or will soon make, lending commitments to support adjustment and debt reduction. In assessing prospects, it is useful to outline three general approaches to the issues and the problems each raises.

First, the OECD governments could take a hands-off position. In that case commercial banks would intensify their efforts to reduce their exposure. This was a policy that served them reasonably well for a time when choices were restricted to damage-limiting alternatives. Capital positions desperately needed strengthening, and wide differences in the interests and strategies of the many banks involved inevitably led to lowest common denominator agreements. This approach has now reached the end of the road, for political as well as economic reasons. Arrearages of all countries encountering debt-servicing difficulties have reached $11 billion. A failure to cooperate now with the performing debtor countries would make their economic prospects bleak, leading to a steady if not rapid increase in arrearages and a further fall in the value of bank claims, which still represent about two-thirds of the total debt of those countries. It is difficult to see how this approach would be in the short-, medium-, or long-term interests of any of the parties involved, including those of the commercial banks.

Second, at the other extreme, a new international debt management institution might be established along the lines proposed by Senators Bradley and Sarbanes, James Robinson, and others. Such an institution would seek to buy up the debt on a selective or comprehensive basis at discounts prevailing in secondary markets and relend it to the debtor countries at these discounts. Such debt buybacks would be tied to debtor country performance as monitored by the international institutions. Henry Kaufman argues that in the end the burden of third world debt will have to be "socialized"; these proposals are ways of doing that.

Whether some such approach will ultimately be necessary remains to be seen; for now the obstacles continue to be formidable. Debt management authorities would need funding from OECD governments to buy up debt, in the form of both some up-front money and much larger commitments to accept contingent liabilities should debtors default on their discounted loans. OECD governments continue to express their opposition to having responsibility for these liabilities transferred to them from the banks. Advocates of this approach contend there would be no cost if the discounts were right, but that assumes the markets would accurately forecast how successful debtor countries would be in achieving the growth necessary to service their discounted debt. Furthermore, this approach requires measures to induce or force creditor banks, dispersed among OECD countries, to sell and write off their claims now—all in the face of wide differences in the tax and legal situations they confront and in how they see their short- and long-term interests in light of these regulations. Legal challenges are also possible.

The third approach—the Brady plan—may properly be seen as falling between these extremes. The plan maintains the cooperative stance of linked responsibilities among debtor countries, banks, international institutions, and governments that has characterized international debt strategy since 1982. Official financial support for debt reduction not only expands the menu of voluntary market-based options elaborated under the Baker initiative, but also provides the World Bank and the IMF with a powerful new means for encouraging policy reform. This financial support in fact represents a limited, indirect acceptance by OECD governments of contingent liability for third world debt, the difference being that this liability flows from the shared commitments each of these governments has in the international institutions providing the funds.

Advocates of a new debt management authority to buy up the debt welcomed the Brady speech at the conference as an important positive development, but essentially, in Senator Sarbanes' words, as "the beginning of the beginning." They questioned whether the potential for debt reduction under the plan would be large enough; the prospect since then for protracted negotiations between debtor countries and banks has added to such doubts.

Nonetheless, writing off the Brady initiative on these grounds is unwarranted. In any circumstances, a growth-oriented resolution of the debt problem will be a slow, long-term process. The Brady reinvigoration of the cooperative debt strategy could certainly move matters in the right direction.

In considering its potential impact, several points should be noted. First, the requirement is not to eliminate debt but to reduce it to a level where debt service is consistent with sustainable growth. William Seidman noted that studies by the Federal Deposit Insurance Corporation suggested that the major debtor countries could service about two-thirds of their present debt. That estimate would be consistent with the fact that a reduction of one-third in their debt or their interest payments would reduce the ratio of interest payments to GNP to where it was ten years ago, when economic growth averaged over 4 percent. A somewhat larger reduction would be required to reach the earlier ratio of interest payments to exports of goods and services. Ten years ago, however, these countries were considered creditworthy and were receiving large capital inflows; now, of course, they must rely more heavily on the increased mobilization of domestic savings.

Second, the next five years or so will be critical, which makes front-loading of debt reduction transactions, discussed earlier, and of new lending the more important. If that can be accomplished and economic recovery advanced, a gradual decline in total debt and a more rapid improvement in debt service ratios are clearly possible. If so, a return to creditworthiness might not be so far behind.

Third, the performance of debtor countries will continue to be uneven, so that financial requirements to support debt reduction and new lending will be lumpy. The Philippines, Venezuela, Costa Rica, and Uruguay are probably ready to join Mexico in negotiating new agreements with creditor banks. On the other hand, Argentina and Brazil, which together account for one-third of the troubled debt, seemingly do not yet have the political structure in place to sustain effective adjustment policies. Using available resources more heavily now to support performing countries would create positive demonstration effects for lagging countries. Should additional financing be required, such successes would provide grounds for using World Bank and IMF resources more intensively and for obtaining support from West Germany and other countries as well as additional complementary financing from Japan.

That leaves open the critical problem of obtaining sufficient cooperation from the commercial banks. The essence of a cooperative strategy is that no major participant can seek to do less in the expectation that others will take up the slack. In view of the difficult and complicated circumstances in which the banks must make their decisions, they may well end up doing too little, too late, to protect their huge investment. If so, regulatory inducements and pressures will be necessary. Otherwise, the Brady strategy and much more will be at risk.

Status, Issues, and Prospects

Paul A. Volcker

The third world debt overhang is a serious problem, indeed a challenge to the country and to the international order. Yet an impasse in debt policy has existed for some months. Whether the means will be found to achieve an orderly resolution of the problem—that is, to help reestablish satisfactory economic growth among debtors and at the same time preserve the stability of the banking and financial system— is an open question.

A disorderly breakdown of the system would serve the interests of neither borrowers nor lenders. It would greatly inhibit prospects for growth in the developing world and political harmony in Latin America.

The three international institutions represented on this panel will have a large influence in determining the outcome. The International Monetary Fund has been at the center of the debt question from the start. It has acted on behalf of the world community in advising and encouraging debtors and creditors alike, which puts it in a rather uncomfortable position. It is the embodiment of conditionality, that is, in pressing for policy reforms as a condition for its support. That is always a hard position to maintain over a period of years. More happily, the IMF couples its advice with short- to medium-term funds to facilitate reforms.

The World Bank has a special mission for promoting development through long-term loans. It has an enormous stake in the resolution of the debt crisis and, as such, is inevitably concerned with structural reforms and gets drawn into broader questions of economic policy.

Finally, the Inter-American Development Bank (IDB) has the special mission of supporting growth and development in Latin America. It has been the focus of considerable controversy in recent years over its precise role, with creditors and debtors having different perceptions.

Any satisfactory positive approach toward the debt problem must have several interrelated elements, all of which involve these three institutions. First, economic policies in the borrowing country must become effective in promoting the efficient use of resources; otherwise neither debt service nor growth will be satisfactory. Policies must be made at home and believed in at home. They are also inevitably going to be subject to international review and scrutiny. In this review, a broad division of labor exists among the international agencies. The IMF emphasizes the shorter-term adjustments, the World Bank the longer-term structural aspects. Overlap is inevitable, and that too is a subject for examination.

Second, debt strategy must continue to be determined case by case. Conditions differ from country to country. That requires particular expertise and discernment by the international organizations in judging country programs.

Finally, the flows of external resources must be sustainable over time. Some of these flows can be official, either directly from governments or indirectly from the IMF, the World Bank, and the IDB. In almost any circumstances, ample participation by private creditors is also necessary. This last element has been most at issue, since it is clear that the assumptions of the Baker plan about the flow of resources from banks have not been met.

A consensus seems to be developing that debt reduction, or what are termed voluntary agreements for debt service relief or forgiveness or write-offs, are also essential to a successful debt resolution package. Some limited steps have already been taken in that direction.

I believe it should be said that debt reduction is not an elixir. If not well managed, debt reduction could be hazardous to the health of debtors and creditors alike. Can, in fact, the value of the debt be reduced in an orderly manner without leading to further, destabilizing rounds of reductions? Can the value of written-down debt be maintained? Would that not require some form of official credit enhancement and therefore a new role for the international institutions? Could they take on this role without jeopardizing the functions they now perform?

Indeed, can debt reduction realistically provide adequate relief when account is taken of a piece of simple arithmetic? Each dollar of debt reduction provides only 10 cents of relief, roughly, in reduced interest. In effect, interest costs are tantamount to the debt service burden, since principal payments are largely rolled over. In calculating how much money may be required, either through reduced interest payments or new credits, one must remember that a given amount of new money is equal to ten times that amount of debt reduction. If it turns out that the problem cannot be resolved by debt reduction alone, and that seems to me likely, then the question of how new money can be effectively raised and the flow sustained is still with us.

In short, approaches to the debt problem must be evaluated by their implications for the resumption of normal credit flows in the future and their effect on economic growth. This question also has been with us from the start, and we must continue to face it.

Barber Conable

We meet in an atmosphere of expectancy—as the existing consensus on debt is reviewed by popular demand. Everything is on the table, and many political and economic diagnosticians are calling for major surgery. Nonetheless, we should not cut the heart out of the Baker plan, because its vital parts—policy reform, economic growth, and long-term investment—are still needed to keep the patient alive. These three items continue to be essential, whatever else we do.

The World Bank has been heavily involved in the debt problem. As a result of that experience, we believe a sustainable debt plan should include the following elements:

—The plan must differentiate on the basis of performance. This is another way of saying that it must encourage developing countries to initiate and sustain economic reform programs for growth. Debt reduction based on unchanged debtor country policies is a waste of time. To cancel debt without changing the policies that created it would incur risk without the hope of reward.

—It must be evenhanded, not in being available to all countries but in being available to all those that accept the obligations of self-help, sound management, and the financial responsibility that will make the plan effective and enable it to succeed.

—It must be designed to accelerate the return to creditworthiness. That should be its goal, because development requires a large volume of investment, which will be difficult to achieve if the drying up of new money from the international community persists. Reducing or even abolishing debt without reestablishing the conditions for satisfactory growth would be a Pyrrhic victory, for it would mean losing the battle against poverty.

—It must be flexible enough to be adaptable to the wide diversity of conditions among developing countries and large enough to reduce debt service significantly.

—It must be wisely implemented by knowledgeable people who don't send the wrong signals or create the wrong precedents. The best chance for success must be taken first so as to build momentum for the learning process.

—It must not gravely weaken the financial position of the commercial banks or the multilateral lending institutions, thus dissipating the capital they need to carry out their primary responsibilities. The objective is to expand, not shrink, the global economy.

Mexico is a good place to start. It has demonstrated a willingness to undertake major reforms and has lived up to its obligations. Mexico's debt is very large, but so is its potential. In return for maintaining and deepening the economic policy changes and the structural adjustments Mexico has put in place in the past five years, the international financial community should help to give Mexico a wider than usual range of options to finance external capital requirements over the next several years. Such options might include the following:

—increased possibilities for debt reduction by swapping bank loans for long-term bonds at a discount;

—exit bonds issued at below-market interest rates with whatever feasible features will make them attractive;

—substantial debt equity swap programs;

—strong adjustment financing support from multilateral agencies; and

—measures by industrial country governments to facilitate regulatory, tax, and trade improvements that could encourage private sector investment and thus give the Mexican economy new potential for growth.

One word of warning: Mexico will need new money even after

significant debt reduction. Financing gaps cannot be filled by magic, and adjustment needs support. The World Bank will do its share in Mexico as in other countries committed to the path of reform. But the World Bank cannot do the job alone.

If this view of the problem does not sound sufficiently idealistic, I remind you of two characteristics of idealism:

Bill Buckley said, "Idealism is fine, but as it approaches reality the cost becomes prohibitive."

John Galsworthy said, "Idealism increases in direct proportion to one's distance from the problem."

Michel Camdessus

Where are we heading as things now stand? In the absence of major financial market disturbances, and on the assumption that industrial country growth is sustained at about 3 percent a year, work recently done by the IMF staff suggests that continued adjustment efforts in countries with debt problems could permit a moderate recovery in their output growth over the next three to five years—possibly to some 4 percent a year—and a gradual decline in their debt-to-export ratios.

Welcome as that would be, growth would remain below rates achieved in the 1970s. By 1993 per capita gross domestic product would barely have regained its 1980 level. More to the point, the resources from that growth which could be devoted to meeting *domestic* needs, including investment, would for many countries continue to be meager. Indeed, a prime concern is that the sheer magnitude of foreign debt could continue to impede the mobilization of domestic resources, discourage the repatriation of flight capital, and undercut adjustment efforts.

To improve the prospects for economic growth, greater cohesion is urgently needed in the response of all parties to the debt problem. The task is to strengthen the ability *and* the willingness of debt-troubled countries to sustain and, as necessary, reinforce efforts to grow out of their debt burdens. Such efforts are extremely difficult, as the unrest in Caracas in March demonstrated. Yet they are essential.

From the outset, countries prepared to embark on strong programs need to be able to count on alleviating the present drag of debt service payments on their adjustment efforts. New credits are one means for doing so and will continue to be indispensable. But in many cases mutually agreed initiatives to reduce the stock of debt are also appropriate. Existing options here clearly need to be built upon. Their *immediate* cash-flow benefits to indebted countries, however, should not be exaggerated. Indeed, additional measures to provide more tangible debt service relief may need to be considered in some instances.

All this is essentially a matter for creditors and debtors to decide. And the composition of financing packages will obviously vary from case to case. In any event, it is necessary to speed up decisionmaking, since protracted negotiations endanger the adjustment process, even where public contributions are part of the program.

All in all, the debt strategy needs to be given a second wind and broader scope. Governments could help, in particular, by removing legal, tax, and regulatory impediments that unduly hamper more imaginative financing approaches. The Fund, for its part, more than ever has a key role to play in providing policy advice, extending credit, and mobilizing other financial support. To the extent we can— and the size of quotas largely determines our capacity to help—we stand ready to tailor traditional functions of support to the needs of the evolving situation.

Fortunately, a great deal is already in place, thanks to the work done in recent months.

—We are now able to provide support effectively in a medium-term as well as in a short-term framework; this was the purpose of the revitalization of our Extended Fund facility.

—We are now able to protect our programs against unforeseen shocks, including increases in international interest rates; this was the purpose of the creation of a contingency financing mechanism.

—The financing we can provide will now be substantially reinforced by bilateral contributions; this was the purpose of the proposal of the government of Japan to undertake parallel lending.

—Finally, in April 1988 our governors agreed that "with strong adjustment programs, more Fund resources should, where appropriate, be made available by increasing actual access within current limits and that, in exceptional circumstances, access might extend beyond those limits."

The importance of these changes has possibly not been fully perceived. As a matter of fact, we could not have been so responsive in recent weeks to the plight of Venezuela had it not been for these far-reaching reinforcements of our instruments and our ability to react.

Among ways in which our work is also tending to develop, let me mention our assistance in analyzing countries' medium-term economic and external financing prospects, an essential function in facilitating negotiations between debtors and creditors on the type and terms of financing that would be appropriate; in catalyzing financing for debt reduction operations; and in helping, as a depository institution, through trust or similar accounts, to channel financing for debt buybacks or for the putting aside of resources to secure interest on debt for debt exchanges. I believe the Fund, through all these possibilities, can help to reinvigorate the process.

As a final word, I would like to stress that a successful reduction of the debt problem requires a good economic environment in the industrial countries: steady growth, lower inflation, and open trade markets. The industrial countries will need to sustain their individual and collaborative efforts to reduce domestic and external imbalances, and all countries will need to come to early agreement in the Uruguay Round of trade negotiations. For its part, the Fund will continue to support the efforts of the principal industrial countries to promote economic collaboration and will continue to encourage sound economic policies and trade liberalization through its surveillance activities.

Enrique V. Iglesias

This issue has been on the table and uppermost in our minds for a long time. I propose to concentrate on the Latin American debtor countries, whose economies are going through their most critical period since the crisis of the 1930s. For the region as a whole, per capita income has dropped more than 6 percent below what it was in 1980. Inflation is rampant, and investment is 25 percent less than it was in 1980.

Undoubtedly the Latin American economic crisis is structural and therefore consists of more than the debt problem. Nonetheless, debt is at the center of the crisis, both for external and internal reasons.

Based on the experience gained over the past seven years, several points relating to the external debt problem are widely agreed on by Latin Americans:

—There is broad consensus that there can be no solution to the problem without the resumption of satisfactory levels of long-term investment and economic growth.

—Although general guidelines and plans are required, the case-by-case approach is the only practical way to deal with the problem.

—No solution is possible without a sustained flow of fresh resources from abroad, coupled with a dramatic increase in domestic savings— that is, in the mobilization of domestic resources for domestic investment.

—The market has demonstrated a remarkable capacity to resolve some aspects of the problem, and its capacity to develop innovative approaches has by no means been exhausted.

No long-term solution is possible without sustained internal structural reform over the medium term. Short-term policy options will not work. Medium-term programs are necessary to address the issues and to harvest the results.

In recent years very few countries have been able to achieve sustained growth, economic stability, and the orderly servicing of debt. Reasons for failure differ among countries. However, two factors have been overriding. First, structural adjustment policies have not been sufficiently solid, sustained, and consistent. Second, the international environment has not been supportive. I refer to adverse trends in the terms of trade, the flow of financial resources, and interest rates. In regard to this last point, increases in interest rates in the last twelve months have increased Latin America's annual debt servicing costs by more than $12 billion.

The negative transfer of resources from Latin America to the industrial world is the key issue. In the past seven years $180 billion has been transferred abroad, with profoundly disturbing effects on the adjustment policies and the social and political environment of the region. A transfer of resources of this magnitude has restricted imports and depressed investment for countries restructuring their economies, and in the process has increased the political cost of undertaking reforms. It has also placed excessive pressure on structurally weak fiscal accounts, which in any event are difficult to strengthen quickly. This in turn has pushed up internal interest rates and inflation and thereby depressed needed public investment. On the other hand, foreign exchange constraints, the collapse of public investment, and inflationary pressures have adversely affected the expectations of the private sector and inhibited the mobilization of domestic capital. Finally, the outward transfer of resources has given rise to steep discounts on foreign debt in secondary markets, thus serving as a strong disincentive for new lenders and investors to commit new funds in Latin America.

In essence, we must now move from the approach based on a liquidity explanation of the debt problem to one based on a solvency explanation. The problem is general and systemic in nature. New approaches are urgently needed.

Consideration of policy revision comes at a time characterized by two elements. Creditor institutions have strengthened their capital positions and their experience and thus are in a better position than they were seven years ago to consider new measures. At the same time, stagnation and inflation have pushed the process of adjustment among Latin American countries to its political and social limits. The need now is to focus on new techniques of voluntary debt reduction and on additional options open to countries willing to undertake or to continue structural reforms.

Debtor countries must redouble their efforts to pursue macroeconomic and sectoral reforms in their economies so as to promote the recovery of their depressed rates of investment in human and physical capital and to enhance the prospects for achieving modern and democratic societies. All this takes time. Medium-term programs are necessary in order to escape from the tyranny of short-term strategies, which are dominated by survival considerations.

On the other side, creditor countries and creditor institutions must also redouble their efforts to create a more propitious external environment for debtor countries, so that the internal push for reform and restructuring does not lose momentum. Most countries of the region are carrying out strong measures to adjust their economies and honor their debts. They need the financial and economic support of the industrial countries.

After many years of adjustment, political leaders in debtor countries require positive results to legitimize their drive toward change and modernization before public opinion. An expansion of the present menu of options, including debt reduction, is not only needed for itself but will also help politically. I am persuaded that such measures will advance the political and economic objectives of a modernizing Latin America, as well as advance the long-term interest of creditor countries and institutions and the financial health of the world economy.

General Discussion

Volcker, as chairman and interlocutor of the panel, pointed out that each of the panelists had cited the policies of the borrowing countries as a central issue for a satisfactory resolution of the problem. While a number of factors have affected the success of those policies, some not under the control of the borrowing countries, the record over the past six or seven years has been mixed at best. Very few countries have in fact achieved the holy trinity of sustained growth, stability, and orderly debt management. He asked each of the heads of the international financial institutions to assess the direction and progress of policy reform in Latin America over these years and to say, from their perspectives, what approaches might now encourage further constructive changes.

Iglesias said the changes taking place in Latin America have been dramatic and in many respects surprising.

First, on the macroeconomic side, there is a growing consciousness of the need to adopt consistent macroeconomic policies. The results may take time to become manifest, but the sensitivity to that issue is completely new in Latin America.

Second, the drive to increase exports is strong. Latin America is becoming outward looking, as shown by the export performance of Brazil, Mexico, Colombia, Chile, and others. Changes have been enormous, including the dismantling of barriers and the opening of Latin America to a more competitive international environment.

Third, the program of reform in the public sector is an ongoing fact. There is widespread recognition that government itself is a large part of the problem and that much of the crisis is basically a crisis of the public, rather than the private, sector. The heart of the problem is taken to be the reform of government, not only in respect to controlling deficits but also to reducing the size of government and correcting deficiencies in government operations. The trend toward privatization is continuing and strong in many countries.

In sum, many structural elements are changing, but the process requires time, and time is perhaps in the shortest supply of all.

Camdessus agreed that a kind of silent revolution is taking place in Latin America. Five years ago the prevalent economic doctrine was inward looking, stressing the role of the public sector to promote investment whatever the cost in inflation. No country is now on that course. Each recognizes the need to open its economy and to reduce the size of the deficit and the public sector. This is an important positive element in the situation.

After six or seven years, however, fatigue has set in. Despite improvement on the external side of these economies, adjustment is less satisfactory on the internal side, particularly for fiscal policy. Internal political pressures, moreover, result in the postponement of indispensable reform measures in order to avoid the kind of time bomb that recently exploded in Caracas.

Consequently, even if the orientation is now much better, the obstacles to action are very strong. Conditionality can facilitate the process of adjusting policies, but a political commitment is essential. In this connection, governments need a minimal critical mass of financing to manage the initial political reactions to change. They need at the outset the certainty that they will be supported. That being said, Camdessus would agree that the adjustment process is on its way. It can be speeded up, and means should be found to help make that possible.

Conable noted that policy reform has been a special problem in Latin America because the region enjoys relatively higher living standards than the rest of the developing world. There are perhaps 90 million people living in absolute poverty in Latin America as against 280 million in Africa and 600 million in Asia. Human and material resources are considerably greater in Latin America than in the rest of the developing world. Policy can therefore make more of a difference. Because of poor economic policies in Latin America, debt has become the large problem that it is. Furthermore, the makeup of this debt creates complications because three-fourths is owed to commercial banks and not to official lenders, while in most of the poorer parts of the developing world industrial country governments are the predominant creditors.

One of the most encouraging features of the past decade has been the emergence of a consensus, not just in Latin America but in other debtor countries, that greater efficiency in the use of resources is the essential basis for resolving both development and debt problems. That proposition is now accepted in Latin America as it is in Africa. In Africa, more than twenty-five countries have come to the World Bank to say that they recognize the need to adjust their economies; they ask how it can best be accomplished.

Latin American countries are participating in this process to varying degrees. There are trouble spots, but major adjustment programs are under way in most countries. Where they have been consistently implemented, a turnaround is occurring. As a result, even though recovery is far from complete, projections show that growth-oriented adjustment with full debt servicing is possible in principle.

Pessimism is still warranted because of the continued burden of debt. That is why additional measures must be taken. Such measures, however, must be grafted onto a continuing policy framework that needs to be sustained and based on economic efficiency, leading to the recovery of satisfactory economic growth, which ultimately has to be the answer to the problem.

Volcker pointed out that the consensus expressed by the panelists that policies are moving in the right direction is inconsistent with the indifferent results being achieved. Is it largely a matter of time? Is the rest of the world not growing fast enough or keeping markets sufficiently open? Has external financing failed to constitute a critical mass—not enough to spur satisfactory growth and investment and at the same time to provide psychological and political support for the necessary policy measures?

Which theory of financial support is right: to keep capital flows on a short leash so as to encourage change because change will be the more necessary; or to be more liberal so as to underwrite more investment and buttress political support for change?

Finally, how large is the needed critical mass of financing? Camdessus presented a baseline projection for achieving 4 percent growth over the next few years, which understandably he portrayed as unsatisfactory. Does that assume new impetus on external financing or limping along at recent levels?

Camdessus said that the Fund's projection of 4 percent growth assumes no substantial change in the rate of lending to debtor countries or in the scale of debt reduction. In his view, additional financial support and the front-loading of policy improvements would make it possible to raise the feasible level of growth to at least 5 percent. The economic potential exists if policy obstacles to growth are removed.

Conable argued that the size of the package or of the critical mass is not as important as how funds are invested. For example, if investment is made in trade liberalization to increase competition, synergistic effects are set in train that make the money go further than if it was invested in a large project. Quality is as important as quantity in Latin America, because it determines the efficiency with which a given volume of capital is used for investment.

Iglesias commented that estimating the critical mass of capital is difficult. What is needed is to reverse the present transfer of resources out of Latin America—to provide enough fresh money to improve creditworthiness. In essence, the aim is to restore a situation of growth and stability so as to reestablish the traditional sources of financing: private capital, the reversal of capital flight, and foreign investment. A tremendous push from external financing would stimulate and support internal efforts to restore creditworthiness and with it the traditional sources of financing.

Volcker, in referring to a tremendous push from external financing, asked why that could not result from the repatriation of capital. Citizens of heavily indebted countries hold very large amounts of capital abroad. Why could they not supply the needed impetus by bringing that capital back to their own countries for investment?

Iglesias answered that this is one of a number of vicious circles that have to be broken. If growth and stability are not present, it becomes difficult to persuade those holding capital abroad to invest at home. An external push is needed to improve the environment, which then would induce foreigners and nationals to invest.

Conable said it is easy to inveigh against capital flight, but it is a natural phenomenon. If policies are bad, holders of capital, domestic or foreign, will invest elsewhere—that is, where they believe a profit can be made. Capital flows are voluntary; they move toward favorable economic environments and away from unfavorable economic environments. Capital cannot be ordered back. Furthermore, once out of the country it is the harder to get it back. Consequently, incentives have to be strong and to look durable.

Capital flight is certainly a very serious problem in Latin America. The World Bank has sought to address the problem specifically through a new agency, the Multilateral Investment Guaranty Agency, which insures investments in the developing world against noncommercial risks. Citizens of a developing country can go to MIGA and get insurance against noncommercial risks for the return of capital to their own country. That option should have some impact on investors concerned about the basic stability of their country.

Camdessus, recalling the experience of France, which is also a Latin country, shared the difficulties expressed by Iglesias about repatriating capital. Policies have to convince investors—national and foreign alike. Experience shows that in Latin countries foreign investors frequently are more willing to give the benefit of the doubt to new government policies than are the citizens of those countries. When an adjustment program was launched in France in 1982–83, repatriation of capital took much longer than had been expected because investors wanted to see if the politicians really meant business. The quality of investments is essential but so is external support, which lends credibility to the program. Investors prefer having the company of other investors rather than being the first.

The practical conclusion to draw from this experience is that repatriation of capital will be a financing element of the medium-term programs but not part of any front-loaded packages. Capital flight will be reversed when the adjustment program is seen to be successful. In this connection, conditionality matters. With it international support can be front-loaded and phased with the progressive implementation of policy, and indeed with what should be expected in the materializing of flight capital.

Conable added that the International Finance Corporation of the World Bank does a considerable amount of direct investment in Latin America. It tries to syndicate those investments so as to attract local investors and provide a Good Housekeeping seal of approval for foreign investors as well. Sometimes that helps. Generally, however, money will flow as a response to the right policies sustained over a period of time. Patience is necessary.

Volcker described the panelists as saying that establishing the right policies is crucial but that even with such policies in place people abroad might have to put the first nickel in the slot to get the music going. He then turned to the issue of voluntary debt reduction and asked whether the multilateral institutions are volunteering to be part of the process.

Conable replied that the World Bank wants to use its capital as effectively as possible, seeking catalytic effects. In general, the Bank believes its comparative advantage lies in direct lending for investment and for adjustment.

Camdessus characterized debt reduction operations, buybacks or other forms, as a good investment for debtor countries, possibly the best they can make financially. Hence it makes sense to support such operations. The IMF believes it can play a catalytic role in this process. It is prepared to provide support to countries that have devoted part of their own reserves to properly designed debt reduction programs. The Fund is also a depository institution, with expertise in managing trust and administrative accounts. It can be useful as well in the securitization of new debt. While it can play a role in these respects, the essential decisions have to be made by the borrowing countries and their creditor banks.

A questioner asked Iglesias to address the problem of corruption as an obstacle to achieving the necessary levels of investment in Latin America.

Iglesias pointed out that Latin America does not have a monopoly on corruption, but he agreed it is an important issue that has to be addressed as part of an effective policy package. Policy instability is a major source of corruption because it creates speculative movements that feed pervasive trends in societies. Restoring growth and stability is an important ingredient in creating an atmosphere that will prevent or reduce corruption.

C. Fred Bergsten, referring to the question of how much external capital might be needed, suggested a target of eliminating the present net negative transfer out of Latin America over the next three or four years. The net negative transfer is now running at $30 billion to $40 billion a year, depending on what group of countries is being examined.

As a rule of thumb, every $10 billion reduction in that net transfer will permit an additional percentage point of economic growth for the debtor countries, other things equal. By eliminating this negative transfer over the next three to four years, the baseline growth rate of 4 percent projected by the Fund could be increased gradually to, say, 7 percent by 1992. Specifically, he would like to see a gradual increase in new capital and reduced interest payments that will eliminate the present net outflow of resources from the region. He believes such a target is both desirable and feasible in putting together a package of new measures. He asked whether the panelists considered such a goal to be reasonable.

Conable said the negative transfer is made up of many elements. Impediments to trade, for example, contribute to negative transfers as would a shrinking global economy. Also in the case of World Bank loans, when borrowers fail to meet conditions, the level of lending declines, which affects the net resource transfer position. A decline in net transfers would be helpful at present, but the elements contributing to it are more complicated than a simple statement of the concept suggests. Clearly, basing the goal entirely on money paid to banks overlooks important variables that are part of the net negative transfer problem.

Camdessus agreed that a positive flow of capital to these countries is a legitimate objective, which he thinks could materialize over a period of two or three years. On the other hand, average growth of 7 percent a year in this part of the world seems too high because the growth potential of the region needs first to be strengthened by adequate policy reform. Growth of 5 or 6 percent seems more reasonable as a target at present. The net resource flow will also be affected by the extent to which flight capital can be repatriated.

Iglesias agreed with the basic idea that the net outflows of resources need to be reduced. He emphasized that the goal applies only to a limited period ahead. The restoration of growth and creditworthiness will encourage the other ingredients of stability: capital repatriation, foreign investment, and higher domestic savings.

Shafiq Islam asked panel members for their rationale in support of debt reduction. On the one hand, the Baker plan supposedly failed because the banks did not lend enough new money. On the other hand, it supposedly succeeded in that it strengthened the banks and the system by reducing exposure to these questionable loans.

The same feature that led to a failure of the plan is then considered to be a mark of its success. Are we now talking about debt reduction because these countries have too much debt to be able to service or grow out of, or because the banks will not put up new money so that the only solution left is debt reduction, even though new money would be preferable?

Camdessus urged care in not moving rapidly from one fashion to another. For some time new money was fashionable; now it is debt reduction. As a matter of fact, the debate over whether new money or debt reduction is preferable is complex, with no single solution for all countries. A blend of both will probably be needed in all cases. In general, the larger the debt overhang and the longer the time required for restoring the viability of the economy, the less appropriate new money will be and the more appropriate debt relief or debt reduction. Over a period of three or four years the mix should change: at the beginning more debt reduction, subsequently a larger proportion of new money. Here too, however, the approach should vary depending on a case-by-case analysis of the countries' differing situations.

Conable attributed the present emphasis on debt reduction to the inadequacy of growth in debt-distressed countries. That problem applies both to Africa and to Latin America, for different reasons. Low growth in these regions also poses problems for the industrial world. Low growth is due in part to the insufficient current flow of new money, which brings debt reduction possibilities to the fore. New money has its advantages as well as disadvantages. The same is true for debt reduction, the advantages of which must be weighed against potential damage to the international financial and credit systems.

Iglesias distinguished two points in the discussion. In some countries the size of the debt overhang is so large that it is a depressing force because of its sheer weight. At the same time, some banks have come to the view that in some countries debt reduction would be preferable to other alternatives. Our stress should be on the differences in country positions and the need to distinguish by a case-by-case analysis.

John Petty asked whether the Fund's baseline projections of growth in the highly indebted countries assumes a total of $15 billion in capital flows, including both direct investment and new bank lending.

Camdessus replied that the buildup of arrears is a major complicating element in the calculations. In general, however, the Fund scenario assumes no substantial change in the present rate of capital flows to these countries.

Peter Jones noted that twelve presidential elections will be held in Latin America in the next eighteen months. Does not this fact suggest that the international financial institutions should accelerate their programs to reduce the risk that governments, under pressure from these impending elections, will walk away from the internal adjustments that are taken to be critical?

Conable agreed that the political instability surrounding elections in fragile democracies is an unsettling factor. The multilateral agencies, however, are not political institutions. They have to insist on sound investment possibilities for the use of their funds regardless of politics. For the most part they must proceed on the assumption that policy conditions attached in their loans will be realized and sustained.

Camdessus added the plea that those now in power not postpone action because of elections. Postponing action is to prepare a time bomb for the incoming administration, whichever it proves to be.

Jonathan Davidson asked whether the concept of debt-for-equity swaps can be expanded to involve swaps for investments in education, science and technology, the environment, and so on, and not be limited to manufacturing or financial enterprises.

Conable saw nothing wrong with such proposals but was dubious that they would greatly affect the debt problem. Swapping debt for these various purposes is likely to be financed on only a limited scale by those who are enthusiasts for each particular area.

The Situation in Latin America

William D. Rogers

If one word captures the mood of Latin America today, that word is desperation. From Argentina and Chile to Mexico, trade unionists and politicians, businessmen, students and ecclesiastics, all share a growing hopelessness, a sense that there is no way out of the foreign debt trap.

When I speak about Latin America as a region, I usually make some hedging statement about the danger of generalizations. Not today. The pall is common to all the countries of the hemisphere.

Throughout the 1970s Latin America by and large did rather well. There was a spirit of optimism. Growth was strong in most countries. Per capita incomes were on the rise. Health standards increased, education expanded, industrial jobs were up. Those were the flush years. Gross domestic product per capita grew cumulatively at a rate of 3.1 percent a year between 1961 and 1980.

Then international interest rates skyrocketed, commodity prices tumbled, recession struck the industrial countries, Latin American exports collapsed—and the banks stopped lending. For six years Latin America has been dead in the water economically. There has been no growth in living standards. For the region, per capita GDP went down 2.1 percent a year between 1981 and 1985 and has been stagnant ever since. Investment collapsed by about 40 percent between 1982 and 1985.

Throughout the period Latin America has witnessed Baker plans and Cancun meetings, declarations from world leaders about the ominous consequences of the debt crisis, and elaborate schemes by legions of economists and investment bankers. But the people of Latin America have seen no results. Words may buy time. In the end, it is results that count—results in the way people live and eat and learn and work. And everywhere—except among the privileged whose invulnerability to economic disaster stands in stark contras every day to the lot of the common people—life has been gettir worse year by year since 1982.

It is safe to say that Latin America has come to realize that its economic difficulties are not entirely the result of its foreign borrowings. Indeed, there has been a remarkable awakening to the need for adjustment: to bring balance to public sector accounts, to reduce the deadening influence of the state, to open the economies of the region to the world, to reduce exchange rate distortions, to loosen the constraints on foreign investment, and to retool Latin industry and commerce to international competitiveness. The old economic debate in Latin America has pretty much come to an end. Orthodoxy has won—for the moment.

A number of countries, at considerable pain and political turmoil, have begun to turn these rather startling ideas into actual practice. Mexico, Chile, and now Venezuela stand out. They have done so because their leaders have come to the conclusion, as Carlos Andrés Pérez recently put it, that restructuring is in the interest of the nations of Latin America.

But this change has made the absence of palpable results, the lack of any real improvement in the way most people live, that much harder to accept. Those who have borne the consequences of the adjustment programs, and the consequences have been severe, have not seen their incomes turn around, their job opportunities increase, their health standards rise, or their children become better educated. For Mexicans today, for example, it is a given in the national discussion that they have collectively sustained a drop in their standard of living of almost half since 1982.

And it is by the same token an accepted truth in the region that a predominant reason for this decline is the net resource drain from Latin America to the external world, a large element of which, of course, is the servicing of the stock of foreign debt.

Net capital inflow was $38 billion on average each year for the first three calendar years of the decade. Inflow averaged less than a fifth of that from 1983 to 1986. Net transfer of resources abroad *out of Latin America* (capital account minus profits and interest on external borrowing) averaged $27 billion from 1983 to 1987. Estimates for 1988 are $30 billion. The accumulated total of net transfers from Latin America since 1982 is about $180 billion, equal to roughly 45 percent of the total stock of debt of the nations of the hemisphere.

Venezuela's debt service of principal and interest payments in 1985 was 38 percent of oil revenues. It rose to 57 percent in 1988. Oil revenues account for the great bulk of all exports.

The international financial organizations themselves contribute to this net drain of capital. In 1987 the outflow from Brazil to the World Bank, after taking into account all disbursements, was $650 million. In 1988 that figure was three-quarters of a billion dollars. In 1989 net reflows back to the Bank from Brazil—from Latin America's largest economy to the world's premier development finance agency—will be more than $1 billion.

To cite Mexico again, the official view of the Salinas government is that the nation cannot grow, and make up any of the enormous ground it lost in the 1980s, until it reduces the negative net transfers for foreign debt to 2 percent or less of GDP a year from the present level of 6 percent. In short, the choice, as seen from Mexico City, is stark: somehow cut Mexico's debt service load by two-thirds or accept endless economic stagnation and a perpetual decline in consumption and investment. That is also the view in every other major capital of the region.

Responsible leaders have no great admiration for debt service moratoriums. The Latins watched carefully as Peru, which stopped the bulk of its interest payments to foreign creditors shortly after Garcia's election in 1985, suffered a 4 percent drop in economic growth and a raging inflation. Brazil's own experience with interest payment suspension was not cost free either. There is, in short, no desire to organize a concerted default.

Yet in all the Big Four countries (Brazil, Mexico, Argentina, and Venezuela) the situation is deteriorating fast. Each is desperate for or will shortly require emergency financing. Venezuela, which in January suspended principal payments on its public sector debt, and where Pérez's far-reaching adjustment program was greeted by riots and a death toll of 300, is putting the final touches on a bridge loan from the U.S. Treasury. In January, José Sarney instituted the Brazilian Summer Plan to bring down inflation and announced at the same time that the country's reserves were far below what might have been expected from its $19 billion trade surplus; Brazil was therefore concerned enough to begin exploring bridging assistance as well. Mexico had to have the assurance of a commitment of $3.5 million from the U.S. Treasury. And Argentina is woefully in arrears on its obligations. In brief, the financial situation of all four is reaching crisis levels just as the Bush administration comes on stage.

In an eerie way, political change seems to be following the economic trends, with an appropriate time lag. During the early 1980s there was a remarkable flowering of democracy. For a time Latin America enjoyed the best political leadership, taken as a whole, that it has had in this century—more responsible, more firmly in the democratic mold, more respectful of human rights, and more prepared to take the economic measures necessary for modernizing its economies.

The decade of the 1990s, most Latins think, will be quite different. Dissatisfaction with the performance of the economy has produced a new Mexican revolution, with serious opposition to the Partido Revolucionario Institucional (PRI) for the first time in a half-century of Mexican history; a resurgence of support in Argentina for the most unpredictable wing of the Peronist party; and a possible runoff in Brazil in its November election between candidates who may be unwilling or unable to carry out the policy reforms necessary for sustained economic recovery. Venezuela has already registered its response to the new austerity measures, just days after the inauguration of one of the great political leaders in modern Latin American history. A new populism is on the rise. Latin Americans sense that the political ground is shifting under their feet. They are convinced that the present is not sustainable.

Thus there is a crescendo of political opposition to the case-by-case debt process. In Brazil, the only constituency supporting the 1988 package agreement of new money and the menu of debt-reducing measures, which retriggered Brazil's resumption of interest payments, was a small corps of embattled officials. The academic community, business groups, labor, and leading politicians including cabinet members are all clamoring to jettison the arrangement negotiated only last year with the commercial banks.

As luck would have it, in this moment of desperation, Latin America has had a shot of expectation. The rumors in early March of a change in U.S. debt policy set telephones ringing off the hook all over Latin America. Hopes have been raised, suddenly and precipitously, in part because President Bush himself promised a new look at the Latin American debt crisis and made a strong point of meeting Mexico's President Carlos Salinas and Venezuela's Carlos Andrés Pérez early in his administration. These are taken as signs that something new is coming. To disappoint those expectations would only add to the difficulties.

Latin Americans believe that the United States conceives of itself as having a special interest in the hemisphere. They see that the largest single share of their own commercial bank debt is held by

American banks. They have been told for generations that the United States believes its national security interest to be at issue in the region, that it has dedicated considerable sums to the small countries of Central America, and that Mexico, the second largest Latin debtor, is a developing nation bordering directly on the United States, one whose economic prosperity will largely determine the flow of illegal immigration into the United States. So most Latin Americans find it inconceivable that the United States will, at the end of the day, let Mexico, and by extension Latin America, fail for want of financing.

They also feel slightly forgotten. They see that the low-income indebted countries in Africa were the subject of a new debt-relief initiative at Toronto, and they know that the Asian newly industrialized countries are enjoying extraordinary export-led prosperity, largely because of their access to the North American market. So Latin Americans are looking for a U.S. initiative in their region in reaction to the rising storm.

Desperation mixed with expectation is a volatile brew. I cannot recall a more ominous time for the hemisphere since the onset of the debt crisis in 1982.

The need for economic adjustment and structural reform, as I have suggested, is generally accepted by most leaders. But the sense is widespread in the region that even if the countries did everything that needs to be done overnight, which is essentially what Venezuela is trying to do, they cannot go it alone. They need, in their view, financial support in appropriate amounts, forms, and terms.

The central issue, as seen in Latin America, is to bring the net capital outflows down to levels compatible with renewed growth. It is that simple. Both multilateral and bilateral public financing is required, and private creditors above all must play their role. Both sources can contribute to new money facilities and to a broader process of debt reduction. Governments can do more, by improving the regulatory tax and accounting environment for debt reduction, increasing the possibilities for debt-equity conversion and new foreign investment, and enhancing the incentives for capital repatriation.

But the critical test for any program, whatever its twist, is that it reduce the net flow of capital out of the region. A plan which fails that test is no plan. The case-by-case process to date has failed the test. More than a midcourse correction is needed. And for this, the view in Latin America is that there is no substitute for vision and political will.

Perspectives of Commercial Bank Creditors

A. W. Clausen

Genuine progress toward a solution of the developing country debt problem has eluded us. Today one finds more and more commercial banks selling their loans at a discount. Markets have discounted the loans of borrower countries far below actual capacities to service the debts. These countries, however, often receive little if any real benefit from the discounts. Meanwhile the new money needed to help their economies grow is not forthcoming. In short, the debt management process has lost much of its momentum. It is useful to step back to examine what we have learned from the experience of the past seven years.

First, developing countries need to implement economic policy reforms. Help starts at home. Second, we know that developing countries need additional financing for their growth. This requires attracting equity as well as new loans. Foreign investment codes need to be liberalized and state controls over economies reduced so as to attract a greater volume of foreign direct investment. Third, new loans will depend on a cooperative effort by the commercial banks, the multilateral agencies, and governments. Fourth, the case-by-case, country-specific approach implicit in the Baker plan remains valid today. The challenge is to introduce more flexibility into that plan. We need to build on the successes we have had. That means broadening our horizon to consider additional options to the present menu.

Perhaps the time has come for commercial banks to take more initiative. Under current practice, debtor countries come to Washington. They visit the Treasury, the Federal Reserve Bank, the International Monetary Fund, the World Bank, and the Inter-American Development Bank; then they visit other creditor nations. As a result, an economic adjustment program is worked out. The available financing is tabulated. Thereafter, the commercial banks are asked to supply the funds to fill the residual gap.

We commercial bankers need to be more creative, even more

daring. We need to ask whether there are not new ways to assist a select group of the heavily indebted countries. The group I am referring to is those nations that are implementing or are prepared to implement strong economic adjustment programs developed in connection with and monitored by the Bank and the Fund.

What I propose may not meet the unanimous approval of all commercial banks. That would not be startling, given the difficulty we have in reaching a consensus on any program. I may not even have the complete backing of my own government. But I believe we must now seriously consider interest rate relief as an alternative to new money.

This shift in emphasis addresses a point that is essential for lenders and borrowers alike: annual debt service payments need to be reduced and stabilized. Voluntary interest rate reduction should be conditional on two factors: first, that the country is implementing economic reforms with technical and financial support from the Fund and the Bank; second, that debt service relief would be accompanied by a substantial credit enhancement of the asset itself. That can be accomplished through defeasance plans, not only on the principal but also on the interest. In any event, we must pay more attention to debt service reduction as a means of narrowing the financing gap. New money alone will result in a buildup in the stock of debt, with rising debt service payments.

Voluntary debt service reduction programs need not involve a bailout of the banks by the industrial nations. On the contrary, the banks would be making a major contribution—my colleagues might even say a major sacrifice—by reducing the interest rate. Debt service relief does not imply that the World Bank or the IMF needs to guarantee repayment of the obligations to the banks. Nor does this concept call for a new institution to purchase debt from the banks at a discount.

Let me summarize.

—My proposal calls for selective debt relief under the same case-by-case procedure that has been in effect these past seven years. Voluntary debt service reduction would be offered only to debtor nations working with the Bank and the Fund to implement multiyear economic adjustment programs.

—Commercial banks would be expected to draw on their existing loan loss reserves and future income streams to reduce the debt service burden of developing countries to levels that will facilitate growth. The quid pro quo will be the economic policies and structural reforms required to improve debt service capacity and overall credit-worthiness.

—Voluntary debt service relief would be conditional on credit enhancement. Both the ultimate collectibility of outstanding principal and a core stream of interest payments must be ensured.

—Debt service reduction agreements would need to include a recapture clause. For example, when a nation's economic performance in any year exceeded certain predefined thresholds, a share of the additional foreign exchange earnings would be paid to the banks. This would represent payment for the forgone interest income of earlier years.

—Commercial banks would be expected to provide new money in the form of trade finance for participating debtor nations.

—Finally, the governments of industrial nations need to play a more active role in the process. It is important that the tax and regulatory environment be supportive of the commercial banks' efforts to help the heavily indebted developing nations reduce their debt service burden.

As you will recognize, my thinking rests on the proposition that the ultimate resolution of the debt problem for less developed countries will be found in more efficient economies. The efficient allocation of resources is the road to greater wealth. It implies diversification and specialization, more rewarding investment, appropriate exchange rates, and the repatriation of flight capital. As economic reforms take hold, creditworthiness will return as a matter of course. My message to my fellow commercial bankers is this: to improve the quality of outstanding loans, we need to help create situations in which economic restructuring can be promoted and sustained. Voluntary debt relief can make, I believe, a significant contribution to that end.

Yusuke Kashiwagi

We often speak of the third world debt issue. But the problems for the middle-income countries in Latin America and elsewhere are not the same as those facing the less developed countries of Africa and Asia. I propose to focus on the middle-income countries whose external debt burden seems to be hampering their economic development and adding to international tension.

The Latin American debt issue is not entirely a new one historically. This region had a similar debt problem in the 1920s and 1930s. That problem was resolved. What factors, after six and a half years, prevent these countries from getting closer to a breakthrough this time?

The answer is the more elusive, given that the world's economic environment is in good shape compared with what prevailed in the 1920s and 1930s. Economic growth in the industrialized countries is sound and steady. There is a generally strong aspiration for welfare, and there are also international cooperative efforts to roll back protectionism. These underlying conditions should provide a good basis for alleviating the debt issue.

Moreover, we now have the World Bank group to support international development, and the IMF to oversee macroeconomic adjustments. These international financial institutions have played an effective intermediary role for the forty-odd years since the war. The contribution they have made to stability, sustained growth of the world economy, and North-South adjustment is recognized by all. But insofar as the current third world debt issue affecting Latin American countries and others is concerned, these institutions seem to lack initiative and have played only a limited leadership role. They could, and should, improve their collaboration with the private sector to advance matters.

It seems clear to me that the resolution of the debt issue depends more than anything else on the will and efforts of the debtor countries to come to grips with the need for structural adjustments to revitalize their economies. Over the past six years or so, private banks have agreed to multiyear rescheduling arrangements (MYRAs) and to the provision of new money in the expectation that a self-sustaining mechanism on the debtors' part would be forthcoming under the guidance of IMF conditionality. As we reassess the situation, the question is whether and by how much the economic policies of the debtors have improved. Instead, the emphasis is on calls for debt reduction and debt service alleviation, together with assertions that the debt burden is too great to allow their economies to recover.

In the absence of a visible prospect for structural adjustment and the regaining of economic balance by the debtor countries, would debt relief or forgiveness give the debtor country economies a more favorable outlook? Some middle-income countries with no less heavy debt burdens have come out unscathed through their own efforts, without even so much as suggestions for rescheduling or debt relief. The credit standing of some equally indebted countries is still high, reflecting confidence-inspiring economic management and debt service performance.

Some of the difficulties are in our own countries. Differing tax systems, accounting rules, and regulatory guidelines among the industrialized countries sometimes act to discourage banks from helping the heavily indebted middle-income developing countries with new credits or market-based debt reduction. I strongly urge the early improvement and reform of such tax treatment, accounting practices, and regulatory restraints, for they are of special importance to the private sector in sustaining the necessary flows of new capital to debtor countries.

Also, adequate monitoring and strict enforcement by the Fund and Bank are absolutely necessary to ensure the full implementation of macroeconomic and structural adjustment programs, within agreed time schedules. That goes for both partial and full debt relief. In fact, the roles of the Fund and Bank need to be looked at afresh from this angle. It is up to them to assess carefully the rates, amounts, and conditions of debt reduction to ensure fair treatment among the debtor countries.

Moral hazard is present in any debt-relief scheme. I believe that the international financial institutions should be asked to watch carefully to prevent anyone from gaining debt relief by precipitating or aggravating a critical situation. Just as important is the prevention of capital flight to ensure that any debt reduction would really benefit the economy. The total long-term debt of the Latin American countries to the private sector is $410 billion, but the total overseas deposits amount to $300 billion. Monitoring should be a role for the international institutions.

Having said all that, I wish to speak bluntly. More debt reduction or debt relief will not solve the debt issue so long as the underlying issues remain unaddressed: the lack of self-supporting effort and malfunctioning domestic systems, including failures in market mechanisms, ineffective tax systems, large budget deficits, and restrictive regulation of private investment. Future measures for resolving the debt problem should be based on a recognition of this situation and provide for improvements.

The restructuring efforts of the debtor countries have not borne fruit in the last six years, and despite their past cooperation and support, the private sector creditor banks have remained largely unrewarded. Creditors and debtors clearly show signs of debt fatigue. The so-called free riders and cheap riders have grown in number in the United States and Europe, while Japanese banks have gone along with an unsatisfactory situation. However, there is a growing sentiment in Japan that this state of affairs has become increasingly unfair and unsustainable. Obviously there is a limit to private endeavors if prudent banking considerations are taken into account. In the recently concluded Brazilian package, only 308 out of some 700 banks and other institutions participated. As a result, the share of the Japanese banks increased from 14.5 percent to 19.8 percent of the total. Today only about 100 top international banks seem inclined to go along in this credit exercise in the interest of international cooperation.

I am aware of the opinion that under existing conditions debt reduction is the key to the middle-income debt problem. This solution is heard not only from the debtor countries but from academics, politicians, and even businessmen. They cannot mean unilateral debt repudiation, for that would make debtor country recovery extremely unlikely if not impossible. Similarly, across-the-board debt forgiveness is simply not a conceivable option. The advocates of debt reduction have in mind, as I understand it, market-based measures in which creditors take part voluntarily. I am not opposed to voluntary, market-based debt reduction. But one should not overestimate its possibilities. Let me elaborate.

If voluntary debt reduction is to be on the debt-relief menu, it must be sufficiently attractive to the market. The size of the discount, assured interest payments, and other conditions must be agreed to by the creditor banks. Private sector banks may not be readily inclined to act voluntarily unless equal or greater reductions are made in the public sector debt, including the debt held by international financial institutions. It would be necessary to have menu options to allow for the widest possible participation and to have ways to penalize free riders. Even so, I believe that the amount by which principal could be reduced by voluntary debt reduction would be relatively small as would the relief on servicing the debt. If, on the other hand, a big discount is allowed or interest payments are not guaranteed, the creditor banks will no longer be willing to provide further new money.

Difficulties experienced by the middle-income countries derive primarily from the shortage of domestic savings; hence the need for an inflow of capital for development. Where can such capital be found? Not in the coffers of advanced country governments, because they face budgetary problems. Official development assistance funds on "soft" concessional terms are not intended for the middle-income group of countries. Even on market-related terms, public funds are still hard to come by in light of the budgetary constraints of advanced country governments. Money that should flow to middle-income countries should be tapped from private banks, not from public sector institutions.

The recycling of private funds to debtor countries will depend on a suitable environment. One way for the developing countries to get new capital without further straining the debt burden would be to get it in the form of private direct investment. There should be abundant opportunities. But there is a certain reluctance on the part of debtor countries. More specifically, there needs to be greater scope for debt-equity swaps than at present. But the willingness and readiness of the debtor countries to accept direct investment is indispensable, and this cooperation seems lacking now.

My bank, like many others, often intermediates debt-equity swaps for customers who are creditors. We do have occasions to feel that we would very much like to swap our own claims into equity and thereby expand our investment and our activities in the debtor countries, but all too frequently we have found ourselves up against a wall of restrictive attitudes. Generally speaking, foreign banks are, I believe, in the best position to cooperate and cover the shortage of funds. I personally would recommend more frequent use of debt-equity swaps to help reduce debt.

If for any reason direct investment is not feasible, then recourse can be made to extending private sector credit. However, insofar as such credit can be extended on a voluntary basis, private funds will flow where terms are thought to be attractive and will not flow where risk is conceived to be excessive. In present circumstances, attempts by the debtor countries to get new money at reasonably low costs will require some kind of credit enhancement. That might be arranged through international institutions such as the World Bank, or through industrial country governments or their agencies. A guarantee of 100 percent should not be necessary, but it should preferably be like the 90 percent guarantee provided by the Multilateral Investment Guarantee Agency.

Cofinancing with the World Bank is another choice, but that would offer only a small incentive for private sector banks unless a full cross-default clause is incorporated so that they, as creditors, would be on an equal footing with the Bank.

Another effective way to help provide new money from the private sector would be, as mentioned earlier, to eliminate the international disparity existing in tax systems, accounting practices, and regulatory guidelines. Of these, I want to stress the special importance of more liberal rules for tax-free provisioning. The introduction of schemes to discourage free riders and ensure impartial treatment of creditor banks is also needed. For instance, interest capitalization or some arrangement to automatically defer payment of their interest claims is necessary to penalize free riders.

Let me conclude by saying that a solid ground for working together can be provided only through a consensus among all parties concerned, including industrial country governments, on the points I have raised. Meetings of this kind can go a long way toward providing a basis for such a consensus, and I appreciate this opportunity to make my personal contribution.

William Seidman

I approach this subject as a bank regulator. As bank regulators, we encourage the U.S. banks to establish reserves for foreign debt when needed. We should all pay tribute to John Reed of Citicorp, who took the lead in reserving, even though many in our government and his industry deplored his action.

One cheer for the private sector. Reed's action has laid the groundwork for appropriate public-private action today. U.S. banks are clearly in a better position to deal with this problem now than they were in the early 1980s. Over the decade primary capital in the nine U.S. money center banks that hold the bulk of our banks' third world debt has more than doubled, reaching $65 billion last year.

At the same time, the outstanding third world debt has been reduced by 10 percent. Today, even if those banks wrote off the entire Latin American debt, after tax recoveries none of them would be insolvent. Regional banks have been even more aggressive in reserving and writing off large portions of their foreign debt.

On average, the money center banks have reserves of about 30 percent on their Latin American debt and the regional banks have over 50 percent. This raises an important question. What is the right level of reserving? My agency, the Federal Deposit Insurance Corporation, has spent some time looking at the debt-servicing capacity of various countries, including their export earnings and other factors. We do so to try to determine what level of reserves is appropriate.

Although what I say can only be a best estimate, apparently the largest debtor countries do have the ability to carry debt that is close to present bank reserves for loan losses, perhaps slightly under. While averages and estimates obviously do not provide definitive answers, they do indicate an approach to appropriate overall debt adjustment by banks. In short, present levels of reserving by U.S. money center banks seem reasonable, though certainly not high. Thus, because of this reserving, their declining exposure, and the increase in their core capital, major U.S. money center banks could reduce a great part of their outstanding loans to the largest developing borrowers and remain solvent, though of course less profitable.

The growing strength of the banking industry suggested by this analysis will help facilitate market-based debt adjustments. Banks were unable to pursue this approach in previous years because of their weakened capital position. The Baker plan has given them the time needed to repair that position.

What is needed now are adjustments of debt to levels that can be serviced. Leadership from the U.S. government must make such adjustment appropriate public policy, one even might say patriotic duty. Tax laws must be modified to encourage debt forgiveness. This approach is not a giveaway to the big banks but appropriate tax policy and good gap accounting.

Incentives for partial write-offs and reserving should be pursued through appropriate legislative and regulatory action. Banks and their debtors can then plan strategies for dealing with the debt problem on a case-by-case basis.

If the government gives the private sector the right environment, bankers will take the appropriate action. They will do it because they have no alternative. After all, they are used to managing bad credits in the ordinary course of business. The amount of these debts just happens to be unusually large, and therefore constitutes an unusually difficult problem. Banks know what they have to do, and if the government provides the lead they will do what is right.

General Discussion

Henry Owen, as chairman and interlocuter of the panel, asked whether the changes in the tax and regulatory environment suggested by Seidman will be sufficient to create an environment in which commercial banks are likely to go forward with debt or debt-servicing relief.

Clausen agreed that the banks need an improved tax and regulatory environment. He insisted, however, that they are cooperating even now. In the past twelve months they have come forward with more than $7 billion of new money to third world countries. Those loans are concentrated, to be sure, but their size shows that the banks have not been as laggard as is sometimes alleged.

Commercial banks could cooperate more if they had more flexible options. His own institution would be interested in a trade-off involving a lower interest rate on an existing loan as a substitute for new loans that would increase its exposure to some third world countries. Other lending institutions might also be interested in such a trade-off because all are long on third world debt.

Kashiwagi stressed that regulatory, tax, and accounting practices differ from country to country, which makes it hard to generalize. Seidman had mentioned the possibility of a change in tax policy that would encourage debt forgiveness. To comment on that possibility, he would need to have more detail, that is, to know more about what would be involved.

Clausen's suggestion about trading off debt service reduction for new lending was similar to what Japan's minister of finance, Keiichi Miyazawa, had proposed at the Bank-Fund annual meeting in Berlin in September 1988. As an approach it is worth careful study, but he would want to know more of the details before taking a definite position on it. Clausen's reference to credit enhancement deserves more discussion. If commercial banks were to be asked to reduce debt service for a period, with the balance fully guaranteed by governments or by some suitable institution or agency, that would be a new and perhaps promising situation.

Not enough attention is being paid to new money, principally because the emphasis now is on debt reduction. Yet new money is what really is needed; getting it moving depends very much on the situation regarding regulations, accounting, and taxes. It is not feasible to have a truly comprehensive proposal because countries differ in their systems, but each industrial country should seek ways to improve its own environment so as to enable banks to resume lending—that is, to provide new money.

Owen asked Clausen to spell out a bit more his thoughts on credit enhancement. Credit enhancement by whom, for what?

Clausen said every extension of credit by financial institutions, including development institutions, should rest on reasonable assurance that the loan will increase debt-servicing capacity, that is, create the capacity to service the loan. To reduce servicing costs on outstanding debt, there should be reasonable assurance that the debtor country has a program or set of policies in place that will enable it to make the remaining payments on the debt and eventually to resume full servicing of its obligations. Beyond that—if we are serious about bringing the debt problem under control in some finite period— there should be some form of guaranty of the debt from the industrial countries, whether provided by governments or the multilateral institutions.

Owen, turning to Kashiwagi, asked what measures, other than changes in the regulatory and tax environment, national governments or the multilateral financial institutions could take to create an environment in which voluntary debt reduction will appeal to creditor banks.

Kashiwagi emphasized the responsibility of the debtor countries for providing an environment attractive to investors. This is a prerequisite in the same way that a good economic adjustment policy is necessary. For example, debt-equity swaps have many possibilities. His bank would like to open branches in a number of debtor countries. If it could swap some of the debt it holds for equity, not only would a substantial amount of capital be provided but the new banks would be a source of further inflows of capital.

Actually, there is strong resistance on the part of developing countries to the entrance of foreign banks. He thought this attitude is based on a misunderstanding. These countries need the foreign banks, which, in fact, have been providing much of the capital for development and would do more in the future. But when the banks come to the point of trying to open some kind of financial entity with a debt-equity swap, the proposal is rejected. Such action hardly encourages banks to expand lending in the future.

Owen asked Seidman whether the changes he had mentioned in the regulatory and tax environment were politically and bureaucratically feasible.

Seidman thought that with the appropriate leadership in the United States these kinds of changes can be made. The banks need to know that the public sector is trying to create the incentives for them to act and that the public sector will pursue their interests in dealings with other countries. It is much easier to do something at home than it is abroad. For a private bank, that is doubly true. A combination of public and private action is necessary so that banks will respond because they see it in their best long-run interests to respond.

Charls Walker asked whether the suggested tax changes would require legislation.

Seidman thought that the tax changes made in the United States in 1986 actually penalize banks in that they do not receive a tax deduction when they reserve in part against troubled loans. That is even poor accounting practice. The United States needs to take the lead and get the cooperation of other countries. That will take legislation, and furthermore it will have budgetary consequences—though not substantial compared with the present deficits and much less than will be required to shore up the savings and loans.

Owen asked what the World Bank and the IMF could do specifically to make it easier for the commercial banks to deal with the debt problem.

Clausen emphasized more of the same, namely in pushing for policy reform. Economic policies make a difference; hence the move in the past decade of the World Bank toward policy adjustment lending has been very positive. The two institutions—the Bank and the Fund—are absolutely essential. They are in position to advise, urge, and induce developing countries to adjust their economies. Debt reduction or the lending of new money will not go forward without economic reform, and if economic reform is to be believable, it must be monitored. Commercial banks do not have clout, but the Bretton Woods institutions do.

Commercial banks may not be all that bright, but they have learned a lot of lessons; one is that appropriate economic policies are essential to ensure that their loans will be, or can become, repayable. Commercial banks are not likely to move on anything unless appropriate economic policies are in place and are being monitored and effective stewardship is being provided.

Kashiwagi thought the World Bank should recognize that it is a bank for development, not a commercial bank. It is in the business of trying to help developing countries, not making money. It should take greater leadership than it is now doing to provide new money to the developing countries. The Bank and Fund are shrinking from this responsibility; rather than taking the risks involved in lending, they are concerned that their credits are safe and sound.

This attitude is very evident in the credits to the developing countries, where the World Bank always insists on a preferred status over the commercial banks. Commercial banks have been asked to restructure their lending and agree to postponement of principal payments. Sometimes their interest payments have been delayed. But the World Bank refuses to do any kind of rescheduling and has always collected or tried to collect all interest payments on their loans. In short, they insist on preferred status.

Take the case of cofinancing. The Bank of Tokyo would like to do more cofinancing with the World Bank, but with an equal, not a junior, status. Specifically, it wants to be a full, not partial, participant in cross-default clauses, which provide some assurance on loans, but the World Bank is not willing to afford such protection to the Bank of Tokyo's share of cofinanced loans. These practices make it difficult for commercial banks to cooperate with the World Bank in providing new money. They suggest that the World Bank can do much more than it is now doing to encourage commercial banks to resume lending on a large scale.

Is debt reduction to be another case of asking the commercial banks to take action but saying the World Bank has more important things to do? If commercial banks are to be expected to agree to debt reduction or debt service reduction, why should they be in the junior seat while the World Bank has preferred status and therefore is not asked to participate in respect to its own loans?

He was less critical of the IMF. The Fund has been doing a fairly good job in negotiating adjustment programs and in monitoring them. But the Fund is needlessly secretive about the information it receives from the debtor countries—information about the status of the economy, the foreign exchange position, and so forth. At the very end of the process it gives the commercial banks a report that says, in effect, here is the amount of new money that commercial banks should supply. Perhaps there are some negotiations that are so delicate, so politically sensitive, that decisions must be taken entirely between the debtor countries and the IMF. But surely a large area exists, especially in the economic field, where much better information could be provided and views exchanged with the commercial banks on how to prepare an adjustment program.

Clausen agreed with Kashiwagi's criticism of the IMF in limiting the commercial banks to a residual role in negotiations with developing countries. The international agencies determine the gap and then the commercial banks are asked to fill it. Perhaps the banks should take more of the initiative, difficult though that may be, because they have information and experience to contribute.

On the other hand, he disagreed with Kashiwagi's point that the World Bank should become a commercial bank. There are lots of commercial banks in the world. The Bank is unique. The world economy would be damaged if the Bank became another commercial bank. The Bank has clout and leverage, and gets attention. Its preferred status is essential to carrying out the unique responsibilities it has. It should be a preferred creditor and not just an ordinary bank.

John Petty asked why the World Bank or the Inter-American Development Bank should not buy debt at a discount in the secondary market and then negotiate the terms of a policy adjustment program with the debtor country. If an effective program was worked out, the World Bank would pass on the discount to the borrowing country and take on a new loan for the balance. That would avoid the legislative problem of creating a new entity but would achieve very much the same purpose and broaden the secondary market.

Steve Dizard, asked to comment on the secondary market, said, first, that as far as volume is concerned the market is surely significant. In 1988 approximately $58 billion of loans changed hands. Currently between $50 million and $100 million of Mexican loans change hands each day between willing buyers and sellers. As for the large banks, the net sellers, their financial reports show that many have been able to make significant reductions in their exposure through operations in this market. As for the borrowers, several, including Brazil and Chile, have repurchased billions of dollars of debt in the market.

But there are anomalies. Current yields on outstanding Mexican loans in the secondary market are approximately 30 percent. New loans made this year will have a current yield of approximately 11 percent. One must expect tension between the price of money at which third world loans will trade and the price at which third world debtors can borrow. This problem will show up when we seek to design debt-for-debt exchanges, clearly an important part of the solution.

Edward Fried pointed out that much of the volume in secondary markets consists of transactions at a discount between private buyers and sellers of bank debt. However, the World Bank has estimated that transactions involving debtor governments in this market have resulted in an actual reduction of $15 billion in the debt of these governments. He then referred to Seidman's study suggesting that the heavily indebted countries could service almost two-thirds of their present indebtedness, which amounts to about $300 billion. This would mean that a reduction of $100 billion, or somewhat more in debt, would bring them to a sustainable debt servicing position.

Speculative as that conclusion may be, it serves as a basis for discussion. Compared to a requirement of a reduction of $100 billion or so, the amount achieved through voluntary market based transactions in 1988 amounted to $15 billion, with a saving of perhaps $1.5 billion in interest. What are the prospects for doing a lot more through interest rate guarantees or Clausen's ideas about the banks taking some kind of new exit bond? The Argentine exit bond fared poorly, and the banks are not battering down the doors to take Brazilian exit bonds. In one way or another, he argued, some new element has to be added to get the kind of additional debt reductions that are presumably required. That element probably will have to be some way of guaranteeing interest and providing the means for debt buybacks on a much larger scale than has been achieved so far.

Owen asked the panel to comment on two questions. Should the World Bank buy debt in the secondary market at the present discount rates and dispose of it in a way that helps the developing countries? And are new features necessary before voluntary debt reduction can happen on the necessary scale?

Kashiwagi first corrected the record by noting that he does not advocate making the World Bank into a commercial bank. To the contrary, he believes that as a development institution the World Bank should be able to take on more risk at less cost.

Coming to the proposal that the World Bank buy up debt in secondary markets, he wondered what the World Bank would do with the debt it had purchased. If it were applied to debt reduction, that would be an admirable gesture, but the World Bank says it is not interested in debt reduction.

He emphasized again that the World Bank, as a development bank, should take more risk. Commercial banks, operating under the constraints of the Bank for International Settlement regulations on risk-asset ratios now tend to look for less doubtful borrowers in place of developing countries. That may be good for the regulators but it goes counter to the objectives of industrial country governments.

Clausen said that additional measures will need to be taken to hasten the pace of voluntary debt and debt service reduction. Buying up a country's debt is not complicated. Brazil's debt is on the market, thin though that market may be, and the loans can be bought at 30 cents on the dollar. Brazil should buy up that debt. But Brazil does not have the resources, for one thing, and it may not be able to get out from under indentures or other agreements that limit its ability to use its available reserves for this purpose. Furthermore, commercial banks have an agreement that no bank in a syndicate will pull ahead of another. Waivers are needed to get out from under so-called sharing agreements, and they must be obtained from 900 or so banks around the world. That is a complicated issue, not easily resolvable.

As to whether the World Bank should purchase third world debt, Clausen argued that the Bank was not created for that purpose. Such programs on a large scale could detract from its ability to raise living standards in developing countries and help their economies to participate more fully in the international system and achieve the benefits from such actions. Debt purchase programs have indeed taken place. Bolivia bought back 50 percent of its debt to the external private sector at a fraction of its nominal value. The Bretton Woods institutions ought to support programs on this comparatively small scale and to encourage the commercial banks to do so as well. But for the debts of countries like Mexico, Brazil, or Argentina, the Bank's resources simply will not suffice.

Robert Solomon pointed out that if the World Bank puts $100 million into buying debt at a 50 percent discount, it is, in effect, helping the debtor country by 20 cents on each dollar it puts out. On the other hand, if the World Bank lends that $100 million to the debtor country, it adds $100 million to the net resources available to the country. Would not the World Bank be helping debtor countries more by simply lending the money rather than buying up the debt?

Petty argued that continuing on the present course will not address the debt issue. To be responsive to the world's needs, it is necessary to test basic premises. Buying up debt is a market-oriented approach. It would relieve the debt-servicing burden and broaden the secondary market.

Owen said the problem is that the World Bank is now using its resources to make development loans. It has no large pool of unused resources. If money is used to buy up debt without putting more resources into the bank, new loans must be reduced. Without making any judgment as to which is more important, it is not much of a choice so far as the developing countries are concerned.

Fried said we should look at what happened after the Baker plan was announced in 1985. Flows from the multilateral institutions as a whole—primarily the Bank—have not been much more than $3–$4 billion a year. That was not a notable expansion of World Bank lending, in part because policy reform in the major countries did not come quickly enough to justify a large expansion. With the capital increase, a more substantial expansion should occur, but it will not be on a scale to meet total capital requirements and the level will still depend on the pace of policy improvements in the debtor countries.

During the same period, net flows from the commercial banks declined to zero and last year probably were negative. That is not to make value judgments comparing institutions, but the World Bank and the Fund, as now constituted, are not likely to be the main providers of capital in the future. For the Bank to have a large role in any debt reduction effort, additional resources will be needed in one form or another.

Bill Ryan noted that in considering the World Bank's possible roles in debt reduction, the disciplines of the capital markets should not be forgotten. The Bank is unique in that 100 percent of its lending goes to the third world and yet its securities are acceptable in the world's capital markets. The Bank's AAA rating on its own bonds and the confidence of investors are precious assets that have to be carefully nurtured.

Fred Bergsten contended that the World Bank could sharply increase its disbursements. Whether it should may be at issue, but it certainly can. The way it can is to greatly increase the magnitude of its structural adjustment loans. That should be done only if, by transferring larger amounts, it could encourage much improved policy performance. A bigger program of World Bank and IDB disbursements seems right. Encouraging better policies and increasing financial transfers kills two birds with one stone. That might accelerate the timetable for the next general capital increase by one or two years in the mid-1990s. It has to be kept in mind that in terms of financial transfers there is now a net inflow to the World Bank from the debtor countries. There is also a net inflow to the IDB and to the IMF. In that sense, which admittedly is only one way to look at the matter, these institutions are part of the problem, not part of the solution. They can increase their transfers but should do so only if the debtor countries respond with better policy programs.

Robert Browne questioned the observation that if the World Bank used its resources for buying back debt it would not have adequate funds available for development lending. He contended that to the extent structural adjustment loans go to servicing debt, it would seem more useful to buy back the debt rather than to pass it through in servicing payments to the private bankers.

Clausen argued that policy lending by the World Bank can be enlarged if more countries are ready to implement structural reform programs. He supports structural adjustment or policy-based lending when wrongheaded economic policies are preventing a government from realizing adequate returns from Bank project loans. In a country where the policy framework is not distorted, it will make sense to finance, say, a highway project. It is worth noting also that policy lending risks the kind of reaction that the Fund has encountered from time to time when seeking to persuade countries to undertake necessary but unpopular policy changes. The Fund takes far more heat from the developing countries than is justified, but these can be emotional issues. Still he would like to see the World Bank move further into policy-based lending, using the prospect of accelerated disbursement as a quid pro quo for action on the economic policy front.

Owen, returning to the issue of interest rate reductions or partial deferral of interest payments, asked Clausen a final question. Suppose a debtor country that had agreed to an IMF-approved restructuring program came to his bank and asked for interest payment relief. Would the request be favorably received? Or would the answer be that it could be considered only if the World Bank or some other institution guaranteed that the reduced interest would be paid on schedule?

Clausen said the short answer is that it would depend. Creditors should consider the idea of interest rate reduction not as something mandated by anyone but as one of the options. Whether they should require some form of guarantee or assurance on the part of the debtor or someone else would depend on the particulars of the case.

A Reexamination of the Debt Strategy

Nicholas F. Brady

More than forty years ago, the representatives of forty-four nations met at Bretton Woods, New Hampshire, to build a new international economic and financial system. The experience of a devastating world depression and global conflict guided their efforts. At the concluding session, the president of the conference, Treasury Secretary Henry Morgenthau, described this lesson in the following manner: "We have come to recognize that the wisest and most effective way to protect our national interests is through international cooperation—this is to say, through united effort for the attainment of common goals. This has been the great lesson of contemporary life—that the peoples of the earth are inseparably linked to one another by a deep, underlying community of purpose."

The enduring legacy provided by the Bretton Woods institutions is lasting testament to the success of their efforts. This community of purpose still resides in these institutions today, and it must be drawn upon once again in renewed efforts to create and foster world growth.

The international debt problem has been a major challenge to the international system over the past seven years. This situation is, in fact, a complex accumulation of interwoven problems. It contains economic, political, and social elements. Taken together, they represent a truly international problem for which no one set of actions or circumstances is responsible. And no one nation can provide the solution. Ultimately, resolution depends on a great cooperative effort by the international community. It requires the mobilization of the world's resources and the dedication of its goodwill.

Since 1982 the world community has endeavored to come to terms with international debt. The year 1985 witnessed a pause and a stock taking of our progress in addressing the problem. A new strategy, centered on economic growth, emerged from that view. That strategy still makes sense. Nonetheless, after four years, stock taking is again appropriate. Thus in recent months the U.S. Treasury has sought to look afresh at the international debt situation. What progress has been made? Where has the community of nations succeeded, and where has it failed? Where has success not met our expectations and why? We studied in depth, and consulted widely—seeking and taking into account the views of debtor nations, multilateral institutions, commercial banks, and legislatures. We also consulted closely with Japan and other industrial countries in order to seek the basis for a common approach to the debt problem by the creditor countries.

I propose to outline the results of that reassessment as part of the ongoing process of international collaboration. I hope that the ideas and suggestions I put forth here will provide a basis for a concerted effort by the international community to reinvigorate a process that has become debt weary. It is necessary to strengthen that process without stopping it. In exploring new ideas in the weeks ahead, it is important to continue working on individual country debt problems.

RECENT PROGRESS

We have accomplished much, but much remains to be done. The experience of the past four years demonstrates that the fundamental principles of the current strategy remain sound:

—growth is essential to the resolution of debt problems;

—debtor nations will not achieve sufficient levels of growth without reform;

—debtor nations have a continuing need for external resources; and

—solutions must be undertaken on a case-by-case basis.

Recent years have witnessed the reemergence of positive growth in many debtor nations. In 1988 six large major debtor nations achieved economic growth of more than 4 percent. This progress is primarily due to the debtor countries' own efforts. The political leaders of many of these nations have demonstrated their commitment to vital macroeconomic and structural reforms. In many countries this aim has been reflected in the privatization of nationalized industries. Some countries have moved toward opening their economies to greater foreign trade and investment. Current account deficits have been sharply reduced, and the share of export earnings going to pay interest on external debt has declined. These are significant achievements, the more so as a number of debtor nations also have advanced toward more democratic regimes. This movement has required great courage and persistence. The people of these countries have made sacrifices for which they deserve admiration. The international community must help to transform these sacrifices into tangible and lasting benefits.

Furthermore, a major disruption to the global payments system has been avoided. Commercial banks have strengthened their capital and built reserves, placing them in a stronger position to contribute to a more rapid resolution of debt problems. The menu approach of the current strategy has helped to sustain new financial support while also encouraging debt reduction efforts. The banks have provided loans in support of debtor country economic programs. The stock of debt in the major debtor countries has been reduced by some $24 billion in the past two years through various voluntary debt reduction techniques.

However, despite the accomplishments to date, serious problems and impediments to a successful resolution of the debt crisis remain. Clearly, in many of the principal debtor nations, growth has not been sufficient. Nor has economic policy reform been adequate. Capital flight has drained resources from debtor nations' economies. Neither investment nor domestic savings have shown much improvement. In many cases inflation has not been brought under control. Commercial bank lending has not always been timely. The force of these circumstances has overshadowed the progress achieved. Despite progress, prosperity for many remains out of reach.

Other pressures also exist. The multilateral institutions and the Paris Club (group of creditor governments) have made up a part of the shortfall in finance. Commercial bank exposure to the major debtors since 1985 has declined slightly while the exposure of the international institutions has increased sharply. If this trend were to continue, it could lead to a situation in which the debt problem would be transferred largely to the international institutions, weakening their financial position.

These are realities. They are problems that must be addressed if we are to renew progress on the international debt crisis.

Let me reiterate that the United States believes that the fundamental principles of the current strategy remain valid. But it also believes that the time has come for all members of the international community to consider new ways to contribute to the common effort.

In considering the next steps, a few key points should be kept in mind.

—Obviously financial resources are scarce. Can they be used more effectively?

—Reversing capital flight offers a major opportunity to obtain new funds, since in many countries flight capital is larger than outstanding debt.

—There is no substitute for sound policies.

—We must maintain the important role of the international financial institutions and preserve their financial integrity.

—We should encourage debt and debt service reduction on a voluntary basis while recognizing the importance of continued new lending. This should provide an important step to relying again on free markets, where funds abound and transactions are enacted in days, not months.

—We must draw together these elements to offer debtor countries greater hope for the future.

STRENGTHENING THE CURRENT STRATEGY

Any new approach must continue to emphasize the importance of stronger growth in debtor nations, as well as the need for debtor country reforms and adequate financial support to achieve that growth. Success is possible only if efforts are truly cooperative. To succeed we must have the commitment and involvement of all parties.

First and foremost, debtor nations must focus particular attention on the adoption of policies that can better encourage new investment flows, strengthen domestic savings, and promote the return of flight capital. These are the policies that will foster confidence in both domestic and foreign investors. They are essential for reducing the future stock of debt and sustaining strong growth. Specific measures in these areas should be part of any new IMF and World Bank programs. It is worth noting that total capital flight for most major debtors is roughly comparable to their total debt.

Second, the creditor community—the commercial banks, international financial institutions, and creditor governments—should provide more effective and timely financial support. A number of steps are needed in this area.

Commercial banks need to work with debtor nations to provide a broader range of alternatives for financial support, including greater efforts to achieve both debt and debt service reduction and to provide new lending. The approach to this problem must be realistic. The path toward greater creditworthiness and a return to the markets for many debtor countries must include debt reduction. Diversified forms of financial support need to flourish, and constraints should be relaxed. To be specific, the sharing and negative pledge clauses included in existing loan agreements are a large barrier to debt reduction. In addition, the banking community's interests have become more diverse in recent years, a fact that must be recognized by both banks and debtors to take advantage of differences in preferences.

A key element of this approach, therefore, would be to negotiate a general waiver of the sharing and negative pledge clauses for each performing debtor country that would permit an orderly process whereby banks that wish to do so can negotiate debt or debt service reduction transactions. Such waivers might have a three-year life to stimulate activity within a short but measurable time frame. These waivers could accelerate sharply the pace of debt reduction and pass the benefits directly to the debtor nations. Debtor nations should also be expected to maintain viable debt-equity swap programs for the duration of this endeavor and to permit domestic nationals to engage in such transactions.

Of course, banks will remain interested in providing new money, especially if creditworthiness improves over the three-year period. They should be encouraged to do so, for new financing will still be required. In this connection, consideration could be given in some cases to ways of differentiating new from old debt.

The international financial institutions will need to continue to play central roles. The heart of their effort would be to promote sound policies in the debtor countries through advice and financial support. With steady performance under IMF and World Bank programs, these institutions can catalyze new financing. In addition, to support and encourage debtor and commercial bank efforts to reduce debt and debt service burdens, the IMF and the Bank could provide funding, as part of their policy-based lending programs, for debt or debt service reduction purposes. This financial support would be available to countries that elect to undertake a debt reduction program.

Part of their policy-based loans could be used to finance specific debt reduction plans. These funds could support collateralized debt for bond exchanges involving a significant discount on outstanding debt. They could also be used to replenish reserves following a debt buyback for cash.

Moreover, the IMF and the Bank could offer new, additional financial support to collateralize a share of interest payments for debt or debt service reduction transactions. By offering direct financial support for debt and debt service operations, the two institutions could provide new incentives, which would act simultaneously to strengthen prospects for greater creditworthiness and to restore voluntary private financing in the future. This could lead to considerable improvements in the cash flow positions of the debtor countries.

Though the IMF and the Bank will want to set guidelines on how their funds are used, the negotiation of transactions will remain in the market place, encouraged and supported but not managed by the international institutions.

It will be important that both the IMF and the Bank be in a strong financial position to fulfill effectively their roles in the strengthened strategy. The capital of the Bank has recently been replenished with the implementation of the recent general capital increase providing approximately $75 billion in new resources. As for the IMF, the implementation of these new efforts to strengthen the debt strategy could help lay the basis for an increase in IMF quotas. There are, of course, other important issues that have to be addressed in the quota review, including the IMF arrears problem and a need for a clear vision of the IMF's role in the 1990s. The United States hopes that a consensus can be reached on the quota question before the end of the year.

Creditor governments should continue to reschedule or restructure their own exposure through the Paris Club and to maintain export credit cover for countries with sound reform programs. Also, creditor countries that are in a position to provide additional financing in support of this effort may wish to consider doing so. This could contribute significantly to the overall success of this effort. Creditor governments should also consider how to reduce regulatory, accounting, or tax impediments to debt reduction, where these exist.

Third, more timely and flexible financial support is necessary. The current manner in which "financial gaps" are estimated and filled is cumbersome and rigid. It should be possible to change this mentality and make the process work better, while at the same time maintaining the close association between economic performance and external financial support.

Although the IMF should continue to estimate debtor financing needs, the United States questions whether the international financial institutions should delay their initial disbursements until firm, detailed commitments have been provided by all other creditors to fill the financing gap. In many instances this delay has provided a false sense of security rather than meaningful financial support. The banks will need to provide diverse, active, and timely support to facilitate servicing the commercial debt that remains after debt reduction. Debtor nations should set goals for both new investment and the repatriation of flight capital, and they should adopt policy measures designed to achieve those targets. Debtor nations and commercial banks should determine through negotiations the share of financing needs to be met by concerted or voluntary lending and the contribution to be made by voluntary debt or debt service reduction.

Finally, sound policies and open, growing markets within the industrial nations will continue to be an essential foundation for efforts to make progress on the debt problem. We cannot reasonably expect the debtor nations to increase their exports and strengthen their economies without access to industrial country markets. The Uruguay Round of trade negotiations provides an important opportunity to advance an open trading system. We must all strive to make these negotiations a success.

CONCLUSION

Taken together, the ideas I have discussed form a basis on which to revitalize the current debt strategy. Such efforts can make it possible to provide substantial benefits for debtor nations in the form of more manageable debt service obligations, smaller and more realistic financing needs, stronger economic growth, and higher standards of living for their people.

Working together can bring important progress toward key objectives:

—to ensure that benefits are available to any debtor nation which demonstrates a commitment to sound policies;

—to minimize the cost or contingent shift in risk to creditor governments and taxpayers;

—to provide maximum opportunities for voluntary, market-based transactions rather than mandatory centralization of debt restructurings; and

—to better tap the potential for alternative sources of private capital.

In the final analysis, our common objective is to rekindle the hope of the people and leaders of debtor nations that their sacrifices will lead to greater prosperity in the present and to a future unclouded by the burden of debt.

Perspectives of Politicians

Bill Bradley

As an American politician I have several interests in the debt issue. The first is American jobs. I think it is enormously important that we do not lose jobs in our export sector. The growth of export markets in debtor countries is in our interest; I would like to see debt policies that promote, not discourage, exports.

Second, I have a strong interest in sustaining and expanding democracy in the world. I am for debt policies that promote democracy, not those that make democratic leadership increasingly difficult to sustain.

Third, I am for a stable social structure in the United States. In other words, I am against debt policies that stifle the economies south of our border and cause waves of illegal immigrants to enter the United States.

So, with those three interests as an American politician, I look at the debt policy of the last six to seven years. What I see is that the way we have handled debt policy has brought sizable job losses to our export sector. It has threatened democracy in many of the new democracies in Latin America. And it has created a potential instability immediately to our south that could result in a flood of illegal immigrants into this country.

Secretary Brady has signaled a change in policy on the part of the Bush administration to include debt reduction—that is, interest and debt relief. That is a significant change of direction. The first test will be in Mexico.

Over the past five years Mexico has reduced its internal budget deficit by nearly 9 percent of GNP. An American politician can appreciate the magnitude of the feat, for it is the equivalent of nearly three Gramm-Rudmans. Mexico has reduced its trade barriers by two-thirds. It has sold off a number of public enterprises. It has encouraged foreign ownership. And it still has difficulty achieving economic growth. So I would argue that Mexico offers a major test case for the new policy of debt reduction.

Secretary Brady's remarks include a number of important points. One is that the negative pledge and sharing clauses in loan agreements among banks should be waived in cases of performing debtors. I have been told by people who have participated in debt negotiations that these clauses have been serious barriers to progress. If they can be set aside temporarily, or made more flexible, prospects for real debt relief should be brighter.

The idea of the IMF or World Bank setting aside part of its adjustment loans for use as collateral for exit bonds is also a dramatic new step. The establishment of trust funds by the IMF or the World Bank to guarantee interest payments on restructured debt or exit bonds for up to one year at a time would be a further significant move forward.

In short, my reaction to the secretary's statement is positive. The real question is, will the amount of debt reduction that follows be sufficient and will the mechanism for delivery of the reduction be timely? I think that the answer will depend very much on the implementer of the new policy.

My choice would be to appoint a "debt ambassador" who would spend sixteen hours a day for the next six months making sure that debt reduction does indeed happen. I believe it will take that level of commitment and that level of energy to bring together the diverse elements of the package and to provide debt reduction to debtor countries on a scale that will facilitate job creation in the United States, reinvigorate democratic processes in Latin America, and create a more stable economic and social environment in Mexico.

Paul S. Sarbanes

We have been asked to look at the debt problem from a politician's point of view. I assume this means a somewhat broader view than that of a banker. I would like to do so and then add some comments related specifically to what has been said here.

In Congress we see the debt problem not only as an economic problem, critical as that is, but as one that affects very important foreign policy interests of the United States. It is a potential threat to the stability of the world economy, and it could have serious security implications for our country as well.

In my view the three main issues at stake are democracy and stability in the debtor countries, the restoration of long-term growth, and the reduction of international imbalances. We have a national interest in expanding democracy around the globe. Yet austerity policies designed to cope with debt service requirements undermine the legitimacy of democratic governments and encourage demagogues of both left and right.

As the *Financial Times* put it in a recent editorial, "Increasingly, it is becoming a question of how Latin American governments can retain fragile democracies when their economies are condemned to stagnation through a vicious cycle of austerity and an insufficient flow of external resources."

The Inter-American Dialogue, a group of distinguished North and South American leaders chaired by Sol Linowitz, has stated bluntly that the Latin American debt crisis may soon touch off a political crisis. As governments lose credibility and authority, the appeal of extremist solutions rises, and it becomes the more difficult to take the economic measures needed for recovery and growth.

The festering nature of the debt crisis has meant that energies which should have been focused on the long-term task of economic development have, in fact, been consumed by short-term negotiations over the debt burden. These negotiations have put an unnecessary strain on relations between banks and countries. They have encouraged rigidity and disputation on both sides. How long can banks and debtors keep going at one another before nerves are rubbed raw, precipitating a costly confrontation?

Third world debt also contributes to the broader problem of world economic imbalances. The U.S. trade deficit has been made worse by the collapse of export markets in Latin America, while at the same time progress toward reducing trade balances elsewhere in the world economy appears to have stalled. In fact, Japanese and German trade surpluses are rising again after posting modest declines.

Both the IMF and the Organization for Economic Cooperation and Development have repeatedly warned that these imbalances threaten world economic stability. A resolution of the debt crisis would enable debtors to import again and encourage countries with surpluses to channel capital to the debtors, thus addressing both the problems of development in the third world and the imbalance in the world economy.

Recently we have seen a number of reports from very distinguished groups dealing with the debt crisis. Certain principles emerge from them, principles to which I subscribe.

First, debtor countries, obviously, cannot continue the large-scale export of scarce savings to creditor countries. According to Stanley Fischer, chief economist at the World Bank, "If growth is to take place, sufficient external resources will have to be found for those debtors who are adjusting. They cannot finance domestic investment while making the net transfers abroad that they have been making in recent years."

Second, new lending is neither sufficient for nor appropriate as a solution to the entire problem. Some of the needed resources will have to come from reduction in existing debt. The report of the Inter-American Dialogue to which I referred earlier said, "Creditor countries and banks increasingly recognize that the economies of Latin America cannot be restructured and primed for growth without substantially higher levels of external capital, that the region's capital requirements cannot be met by new lending alone, and that debt reduction is, therefore, essential."

Third, debt reduction means acceptance of losses by the banks. Prices of debt in the secondary market demonstrate that in the market's judgment third world debt is not worth its face value. Public policy should ensure that market-based discounts are reflected in reduced obligations by the debtors. I find it unjust and, in fact, destructive of the process that primary creditors have sometimes taken losses on their loans, while the debtor countries have gained no additional breathing room at all. It seems to me that this connection must be recognized.

Fourth, a new strategy needs to be long term to remove the element of uncertainty that is so debilitating to growth. It must be comprehensive, involving all debtor countries, not merely the large or strategically significant. At the same time it must be flexible enough to treat different countries differently. A comprehensive approach is not incompatible with a case-by-case review. Comprehensive means only that we should approach the debt issue in an embracing way so as to enable all countries to try to move back to a growth path.

Fifth, the provision of new resources, either through new lending or debt relief, must be linked to continued momentum on policy reform in the debtor countries. The real goal of any effective debt strategy is to restart the growth process. This requires both external resources and appropriate internal policies. Whether the creditor banks themselves should insist on conditionality is doubtful. I am not sure that the best way to get the kind of developing country discipline we are seeking is to have the pressure come from the private banks. It is tough enough for politicians to respond to the advice of an international institution, as we have seen in Venezuela.

Sixth, the debt problem is an international problem. I want to stress this point. American banks hold only a third of the loans to troubled debtors. In my view the solutions must be multilateral, not unilateral or bilateral. Multilateral solutions also hold out the possibility of addressing the larger problem of major trade imbalances, which threaten to undermine world recovery.

To the greatest extent possible, debt reduction for developing countries should be facilitated through the recycling of capital from such countries as Japan and Germany, which have large current account surpluses. Such an approach to the third world debt problem may well provide an opportunity for more equitable and realistic burden-sharing, long overdue.

The United States spends 7 percent of GNP on defense. Japan spends 1 percent, while enjoying the U.S. security umbrella. I am not one who thinks the United States should push Japan to rearm. I do think it reasonable, given the strength of the Japanese economy and its large current account surpluses, that Japan should take an important role in addressing some of these economic problems and that this role be played in a multilateral context. Indeed, all the nations that are going to have a part ought to join together in doing so. It should be an international initiative in which no single country seeks to gain trade or other advantages.

The debt problem has festered for years. It now poses an urgent challenge. It threatens fragile democratic institutions. It threatens the living standards of millions of people. It threatens U.S. foreign policy interests. I am frank to say that I do not think Secretary Baker will be able to have an effective American foreign policy in a number of places in the world if that policy does not have an important debt component. Third world debt is an issue he will constantly encounter.

Since the early 1980s debt policy has been largely reactive, driven by the need to contain crises. It is time for policy to take the lead by remedying the underlying conditions that generate the crises.

Let me just comment briefly on Secretary Brady's statement. Paraphrasing Churchill, I think it is the beginning of the beginning. I welcome the Treasury's adoption of the concept that debt reduction is a necessary part of any realistic debt package.

It is difficult to go beyond that because we do not know the magnitudes or many of the details. A large responsibility will be placed on the banks to carry things through. That has been tried these past four years with very modest results. A good deal was supposed to be accomplished by flows of new money. That did not happen.

Obviously what is needed is sufficient reduction of the debt overhang for debtor countries in the course of adopting the right economic policies to resume economic growth. I think all will have to share in the process—the governments, the multilateral institutions, and the banks. Finally, it will require a genuine commitment from countries that have very large current account surpluses and very strong economies but have not as yet assumed commensurate economic responsibilities.

Jim Leach

It strikes me that we are on the edge of a paradigm shift in international affairs, from an emphasis on East-West to an emphasis on North-South relations, from an obsession with geopolitical to a focus on geoeconomic challenges, from concerns with military parity to ones of social balance.

In this context Secretary Brady's speech is to be welcomed. As a reflection of nonideological flexibility and short-term accommodation, it is very impressive. The days of gradualism seem to be over, and modifications in the Baker approach can no longer be put off.

From an American political perspective, it should be stressed that the new president is confronted with a double catch-22 situation. While the international debt problem has grown, the resources to deal with it are smaller. Simply put, in American public life there is little support for appropriating more monies to be directed at third world problems. As we shift gears, we have no choice but to place the emphasis on reducing old debt rather than to raise false expectations that new money commitments are in the offing.

The Brady approach, therefore, quintessentially reflects President Bush's lament that he has a will without a wallet. In this sense it also represents close to the maximum that can be expected under the circumstances.

The precise role of Japan is yet to emerge, although it was slightly hinted at in the secretary's speech. But it is encouraging that the Japanese support the Brady initiative and are willing to augment the resources of the World Bank and the IMF in debt reduction efforts.

It is my understanding that the president raised the third world debt issue as a matter of highest concern when he met with Prime Minister Takeshita and that the prime minister did signal a desire to be cooperative. How forthright the Japanese are on this issue could have a great deal to do with how the U.S. Congress, as well as the executive branch, deals with a host of U.S.-Japanese issues in the years to come.

Speaking as a legislator, I would like to express no sympathy whatsoever for commercial bank regulatory forbearance as a quid pro quo for commercial bank participation in debt reduction. This is precisely what got the American thrift industry into trouble, and it should not be tolerated in commercial banking. Despite, and perhaps because of, the "too big to fail" syndrome, no bank should be considered too big to regulate.

Just as a difference between thrift and bank regulation helped precipitate the savings and loan crisis, a difference between regulation of international and domestic banking helped precipitate the present third world debt problem. The great scandal of the Federal Reserve Board in the last several decades has had little to do with money supply decisions and much to do with imprudent regulation, which had the effect of allowing imprudent decisions on lending abroad.

The reported dispute between the Treasury and the Fed about whether to induce banks to embrace the new approach by forcing larger write-offs or reserving more on third world debt should not be considered simply a judgmental debate. The discretion of regulators is constrained by legal parameters. Here the law is clear. Sections 905 and 908 of the International Lending and Supervision Act of 1983, which I initiated, requires regulators to establish adequate levels of reserves against impaired foreign debt and stipulates that such reserves "shall not be considered as part of capital and surplus or allowances for possible loan losses for regulatory, supervisory, or disclosure purposes."

The Fed has the legal obligation, whether it likes it or not, to go along with the Treasury. The Treasury, for its part, which through the Office of the Comptroller of the Currency has dual responsibility for regulating national banks, lacks the option of giving in to the Fed. There has been only one positive aspect of the failure to date to enforce provisions of the principal statute of direct regulatory relevance: it is better to induce banks to transfer the benefits of debt reduction to the governments that owe it than to private speculators. Congress in this regard ought to make clear its profound preference for the reduction of country debts rather than the simple transfer of bank loans at a discount from one private hand to another.

As for tax forbearance, international banks have always received preferential treatment for tax liabilities, and it is hard to see the social or ethical case for granting more tax advantages. Comparability with foreign laws is always something we should take into consideration, but it is not the only concern Congress should have.

With regard to guarantees, it strikes me that they should only be considered in the context of an international arrangement in which the United States would be a participant but not the exclusive guarantor. Guarantees of new debt issues would appear less compelling than consideration of international guarantees for restructured, substantially discounted, old debt.

The bad news in banking is that things are coming to a head. The good news is that the American banking system seems far more viable today than five years ago. Total developing country exposure has been reduced. Liability is partially reserved and to a lesser extent written off, all linked to the stronger equity positions of American money center banks. The strengthening of bank positions, however, has been matched by a weakening of the social fabric in the developing world, which is now engaged in an unprecedented transfer of resources from the poor to the rich. Here hard-headed bankers have no choice but to heed UNICEF's plaintive plea—that third world kids are dying so as to pay the interest on obligations taken by institutions that are beyond their control or understanding.

In discussions with bankers, I am always struck by the naïveté, if not innocence, of the assertion that the debt problem simply reflects a governmental quasidirective to money center banks to recycle petrodollars and that no one in Washington in the 1970s suspected or warned against looming problems. I feel compelled to point out that more than ten years ago, as a freshman member of Congress, I introduced legislation requiring either an increase in capital ratios for international lending or the application of reserve requirements for international liabilities to stem the egregious growth in lending in developing countries. In hearings before the House Banking Committee my legislation was laughed out of the box by representatives of the money center banks, who patiently explained that sovereign guarantees were stronger than home or farm mortgages, even though no one could explain how a bank could enforce a lien on Brazil.

I raise this legislative anecdote to underscore the precept that capitalists should be held accountable for capitalist mistakes. It was with their eyes wide open, not because of governmental inducement, that international banks doubled third world lending from 1979 to 1982. Thus the U.S. taxpayers should not now be expected to make up for the past mistakes of financial institutions.

Congress must be concerned foremost with the safety and soundness of banks, not their size. Entrepreneurship should not be risk free. Money center banks can no longer duck shareholder accountability, that is, to run the gauntlet of raising money the old-fashioned way, through equity offerings. To the greatest extent possible, the public must be shielded by the cushion of invested capital from either direct bailouts of an industry, as in the S&L mess, or indirect bailouts through intermediary institutions like the World Bank and the IMF.

To date, American money center banks have understandably been concerned that too much governmental intervention could spell policies which could stretch the Constitution. The problem is that a do-nothing approach in Washington will lead to intransigence among borrowing countries abroad, ending in repudiation of debt. The only hope for forging a policy that preserves the banking system as we know it today and meets the humanitarian concerns of the developing world is to create a new government–private sector partnership of hope and reason. The Brady initiative may be insufficient, but it is a giant step in the right direction. It also makes mincemeat of gossip that the Bush administration has no driving vision.

The fact is that our new president has inherited a rather barren plate from his predecessor. A domestic and international financial crisis has been in the making for some time. It has fallen on the Bush administration to act. Within fifty days the new administration has produced a remarkably comprehensive approach to the S&L problem and signaled a shift of gears in international finance. It is not clear that traumatic convulsions can be avoided, but it is clear that the new president has removed the rose-colored glasses of his predecessor and moved with professional dispatch. At the heart of any financial system is the intangible ingredient, confidence, and as a legislator I feel compelled to give the administration all the benefit of the doubt.

People talk about the need in times of political crisis to walk to the water's edge in unity. If the great political crises of the next generation are likely to be of economic origin, we in Congress must work as constructively as possible, together with the executive branch, to right the mistakes of the past so that confidence is maintained in our system and way of life and that a tolerant respect for the opinions of mankind is advanced. Likewise, the private sector, in this case commercial banking, would be well advised to cease hiding behind surrealist accounting and face up to the reality that when tough times loom, greater resources must be marshaled. It is time to back the president.

General Discussion

Bruce MacLaury, as chairman and interlocuter of the panel, said he believed he knew where Congressman Leach stood on the question of the U.S. government's contribution to the debt reduction initiative in terms of additional tax relief or other assistance to creditors. But he wished to ask the two senators for their views about any further part the United States should have in the process.

Sarbanes responded that under existing law there would obviously be some taxpayer involvement because if the banks take a loss, that will be reflected in their taxes. He does not favor changing the tax law to provide tax write-off benefits when a reserve for loan losses is set aside. The act of establishing a reserve does not in itself help debtor countries. At the minimum, if the taxpayer is going to make any contribution to banks, it ought to be when bank losses help to ease the third world debt problem.

The large developed countries ought to be prepared, if necessary, to provide additional support to whatever international institution we are working through so as to enable it to take larger initiatives on the debt issue. He said that at one point he put forward the idea of a separate debt facility that could buy a portion of debt from the banks at a significant discount. If debtor countries adopted the right policies, one could assume that they could then handle the remaining debt. In any such arrangement industrial countries running large current account surpluses should take a much larger share of the responsibility than they have generally borne on economic matters.

Bradley said no taxpayer dollars are necessary. Under the 1986 tax law, a bank can take a loss for tax purposes only when it writes off the loan. Before the 1986 tax revision, it could take a write-off by establishing a provision for losses, essentially keeping the asset on its books. We should not change the 1986 law.

We also need to know what discount is involved in debt reduction swaps of one kind or another. If loans are discounted to their value in secondary markets, no subsidy is likely or even possible. If, on the other hand, the loan is discounted to, say, 90 percent of its nominal value when the market says it is worth only 40 cents, a potential subsidy exists.

MacLaury noted that each of the three legislators has referred to the need for burden sharing, and in particular the need for greater participation by countries with current account surpluses. The focus of course is on Japan. One of the questions raised by the Japanese is that if Japan is to make a disproportionate contribution to a solution of the debt problem, should that not be reflected in increased voting shares in the international institutions?

Sarbanes replied that a disproportionately large contribution by Japan in this instance would help to reduce the inequality that now exists with respect to the security burden. Once the discrepancy between the combined contributions in the security and economic areas diminishes, disproportionate contributions ought to bring with them an increase in voting rights in the institutions. But at the moment, a case is being made for a larger voice in the institutions to follow on an economic contribution, whereas a very large gap on the security side continues to exist and is not being corrected in any other way.

Bradley pointed out that up until now the Japanese have been more willing to participate in a resolution of the debt issue than the United States has. He does not believe that the Japanese are going to be unreasonable in asking for additional influence in the institutions, so he would not jump to conclusions about the need to address the problem of increased voting strength in any of the international financial institutions. The Japanese seem more than willing to be a part of any debt reduction proposal that promises to stimulate growth in many of these countries and to lessen the threat to the world financial system.

Sarbanes thought it might be worth considering working the debt reduction approach through an adjunct of the World Bank or the IMF. There was a special facility in the IMF with respect to oil in the 1970s. Something analogous to that would not raise the issue of voting rights in the World Bank or the IMF.

Leach commented that quite clearly the U.S. debt reduction proposal has received an airing in Japan, but nothing has been fully negotiated. Speaking as a legislator, and thinking in the total context of U.S.-Japanese relations, he believes the debt problem is the foremost economic challenge in the world. If Japan does not respond in a very forthcoming way, it is going to be very difficult to deal sensibly with a host of other issues affecting relations between the two countries. One of the first things with which Japan must cope is its position that no principal can be written off. The second issue is what funds it can provide and in what context.

Sarbanes added that the United States could accept continuing trade deficits with Japan, although not of their present magnitude, if it was running trade surpluses elsewhere. A contribution that would enable Latin America to return to a higher growth path and therefore to resume importing on a larger scale could diminish existing pressures on the direct U.S.-Japanese trade relationship.

Karen Lisaker wondered whether there are not a couple of levers, not involving taxpayers' funds, that Congress could use to advance the debt reduction proposals. Congressman Leach touched on one, that is, the question of recognizing the actual value of third world loans. Since the proposal concerns voluntary debt reduction, one could encourage banks to volunteer more debt reduction offers if the regulatory agencies were compelled to observe the intent of the International Lending Supervision Act in recognizing a value-impaired loan when they see one.

The second lever concerns asset enhancement—providing some sort of guarantee or insurance for the assets that would remain on the books after debt reduction. To avoid contributing U.S. taxpayers' funds to that effort—and Japan cannot be expected to take on the whole burden—use could be made of deposit insurance.

Congress is now considering a markup of the deposit insurance legislation, where Eurodollar deposits already constitute a large part of the whole. These deposits funded many of these now-troubled third world loans. Furthermore, they are currently subject, since Continental Illinois, to the implicit, if not the explicit, backing of the U.S. government. Yet the banks pay no insurance fee for insurance coverage or Eurodollar deposits. Would not the requirement to pay such fees be a justifiable source of funds for an enhancement facility?

Leach was frankly skeptical about deposit insurance on overseas liabilities. First, it would reduce the incentive to bring money back to America. Second, it would put U.S. banks in a slightly less favorable competitive position. But the question raises an important issue, apart from deposit insurance. The international banks—other than Continental Illinois to some extent—have not drawn on the Federal Deposit Insurance Corporation to date. Conceivably they could in the future. One might well craft a statute to the effect that deposit insurance will be placed on overseas liabilities unless banks agree to participate in a program for debt relief.

John Anderson said the focus of the fine presentations by the members of Congress has been debt reduction. If attention is to be centered on debt reduction, what will it mean when a replenishment of the International Development Association (IDA) is needed? And will members of Congress point to debt reduction as a substitute for the normal development assistance appropriations?

Sarbanes thought that would not happen. First of all, Congress did fairly well last year in appropriations for the multilateral lending program. There is a recognition that more, not fewer, resources are needed. There are of course tremendous budget pressures. But the debt problem cannot be solved through the budget; the approach has to be through the private sector. Congress has a problem of not enough money to deal with the development problem. But that is a separate issue, which will not be significantly affected in a congressional perspective by an initiative to reduce the overhang of debt.

Leach added two points. First, it is significant that Secretary Brady said we must deal with the IMF quota issue this year. It had been a little disingenuous for the United States to say that it was waiting for the Fund to come up with a plan, as if the IMF did less thinking about the third world debt issue than the Reagan administration did last year. But whatever the rationale, the Bush administration now has IMF replenishment on the table. That is very good news.

Second, the bad news, and here he differed a little with Senator Sarbanes, is that all indications coming from Congress are that direct foreign aid will be cut. In fact, one of the unadvertised executive-legislative branch differences during the past few years is that, quite literally, the Reagan administration proposed more aid than liberals—that is, the Democratic party—in Congress passed. This year the relevant appropriations committees are saying that about a billion dollars or a bit more will be pared from foreign assistance. The fact is that foreign aid does not pull at the heartstrings of most members of Congress.

Bradley added that if you eliminated the U.S. contributions to IDA, it would be insignificant in relation to debt reduction. If we are serious about restoring growth, debt reduction will have to be much bigger than what is contributed to IDA. The fact is that the disturbances in Venezuela following the introduction of an adjustment program and the 50 percent drop in real wages in Mexico over the past seven years have large political repercussions. Secretary Brady's statement is a recognition that there is a political dimension to this problem to which the United States must respond.

Robert Berg noted that the one area of the world in which relative economic performance over the last decade has been worse than Latin America is sub-Saharan Africa. He asked whether Secretary Brady's proposals would help in any way to get growth restarted there.

Walter Fauntroy saw nothing in the Brady statement to suggest any help in that direction. Congress did include in the trade bill a request that the administration pursue the idea of using special drawing rights—a special issue of SDRs—for the poorest nations, which could then be used for reducing their official debt. The Treasury response is past due. Secretary Brady's statement does not qualify as a response, since it does not address the question of what might be done to reduce the official debt held by the poorest nations in Africa, particularly the sub-Saharan African nations.

Sarbanes said one of the reasons he spoke for a comprehensive approach is that he thinks it is important to address the debt problems of all the debtor countries. We tend to focus on Latin America, but obviously there are problems elsewhere as well. The solutions need to take different forms. The amounts required are different. Who holds the debt is different. For example, debt forgiveness seems appropriate for some of the African countries. Without a comprehensive plan, the apprehension will always exist that what is done in one country will be a precedent for what is to be done elsewhere.

The same is true if the approach centers on a lead country. Whatever terms a lead country gets then become the absolute minimum that the next country will expect. At some point we need to view the problem comprehensively and seek to deal with it—to give countries the opportunity to grow if they follow the right policies. Unless the approach is comprehensive, what is asked of one country, which might be able to be quite forthcoming, will be resisted because something less will be asked of some others.

Concluding Impressions

Jesús Silva Herzog

We have definitely come to a different stage of the debt problem. A conviction is growing that the strategy followed since 1982, with subsequent minor adjustments, needs to be modified and a new reality recognized. Muddling through, an expression much in vogue a year ago, was not mentioned at this conference.

Muddling through provided time and space for maneuver, but it succeeded only in postponing, not solving, problems. As described at this meeting, those problems are not exclusively financial, but have a political element and a clear international dimension.

The situation in the debtor countries is now worse than in 1982. True, six debtor countries experienced economic growth in 1988, but many more than six countries are involved. More important, for the region as a whole the light at the end of the tunnel is not clearly seen.

In the debtor countries it has become evident that it is not possible to resume growth while carrying present debt service charges. The negative transfer of resources is impeding recovery. At the same time all recognize—the debtors, the creditor countries, and the international organizations—that growth is essential if the debt problem is to be brought under control and adverse social and political consequences in the debtor countries kept in check.

It is paradoxical that in this difficult period for debtor nations, a very severe adjustment has taken place in Latin America and with it a very substantial change in economic policy. Dogmas that were constants in Latin American economic thinking for decades have been modified, although with different degrees of intensity in the various countries. There is a growing consensus that change must be introduced in the basic economic philosophy of all Latin America. But the adjustment process has its limits; I believe the debt burden now stands in the way of its continuation.

There is widespread agreement at this meeting that economic reform is essential. The real question is whether it can continue under existing economic, financial, social, and political limitations. I do not think it can without a clear signal of stronger medium-term foreign financial support.

It is useful to review changes in attitudes toward the debt problem since it emerged as a major issue. In 1982 and 1983 it achieved the status of a crisis and was a matter for headlines. Complacency began to take hold in 1984, along with judgments, clearly premature, that the debt problem was over. During the period 1985–87 debt became a secondary issue, except for emergency cases such as Mexico in 1986 and Brazil and Argentina in 1988. Recently the debt problem has again come to the fore, basically because of a growing recognition of the problems depressing the debtor countries and of the repercussions that a postponement of a solution to the debt problem can have in the world as a whole.

My own views can be summarized as follows:

First, adjustment and economic reform in the debtor countries is necessary. Some countries have in fact recognized the policy mistakes that were made during the past decade, some that clearly were a domestic responsibility and some that were in response to negative external events. Both factors combined to produce this unfortunate result.

Second, economic reform has to concentrate essentially on the mobilization of domestic savings. Even under the most optimistic assumptions external capital will not be as abundant or as important as it was before the debt crisis. Thus the stimulation of domestic savings and the improvement in the efficiency of their use are absolute requirements.

Third, economic programs must be seen as domestically made. Resistance to something that can be interpreted as having been imposed from the outside is growing, dramatically so in recent months. How to introduce a local element in the design of economic programs is, in my view, fairly simple, but it will require some change in how the chips are used.

Fourth, while pursuing adjustment, ways must be found to reduce debt and at the same time increase financial flows to the indebted countries. That is indeed a difficult combination, but I believe it can be done. To talk about debt relief or debt reduction six months ago or three years ago was anathema, looked upon as putting serious obstacles in the way of attracting fresh money. Now we talk not about debt relief, but about debt reduction. I am encouraged by this change in basic attitudes and by the fact that many of the positions of the debtor countries since the beginning of the debt crisis are beginning to be recognized.

As a final comment, I would stress that the debt problem is not going to be solved in the short run. It will be with us for many years, and it is better for our societies to understand this. The schemes that have been developed so far will make only a modest contribution, so we should be careful not to raise expectations that, unrealized, will lead to frustration. There is no longer room for taking that kind of psychological risk.

Henry Kaufman

The presentations this morning, the secretary of the treasury's statement at lunch, and the remarks this afternoon have made this an extraordinary day. I was most struck by the urgency expressed by Mr. Rogers and the poignancy with which he expressed that urgency. Later on, expressions of concern about the debt crisis were more muted, which is understandable because officials speak in a modest tone and seek to avoid great excitement.

The secretary of the treasury's statement departed from the previous official view. Indeed, references throughout the day to debt reduction and debt relief, and even a whisper of the term debt forgiveness, were in themselves a far different language from that used to discuss this problem a few years ago.

It is important to recognize that these expressions of concern occur against an economic backdrop that may well pose a further challenge to the debt problem in the next few years. The United States is in the seventh year of an economic expansion; to assume that the business cycle is a concept of the past is to be foolhardy. Sometime in the next two or three years the United States will have a recession. When that occurs, the debt situation will be under additional pressure.

Furthermore, a compounding dilemma faces us. Most industrial nations are moving closer to what I would call cyclical economic convergence. Their economies today are characterized by a capital expenditure boom, a high level of consumer spending, and, with the exception perhaps of Japan, an increase in inflation and interest rates. While it is still unlikely that the industrial countries will all peak at the same time, that possibility has to be raised, and its severe consequences for the debt side considered. That makes it the more urgent to address the debt problem now.

The belief has been expressed today that world financial markets are much better prepared to deal with the debt problem than in the recent past. I consider this a misconception. It is true that third world debt is a smaller percentage of the assets of the lenders, that loan loss reserves are now much larger, and that, as a result, the financial markets are in a better position to accommodate net new lending to these countries. On the other hand, the opportunities for financial market participants to lend and invest have become more attractive outside than inside the third world.

For example, the United States is witnessing an internalization of its financial system. Massive consolidation lies ahead, in which market shares will be at stake. Institutions will merge in order to gain a substantial toehold on the household market, the mortgage financing market, and the business financing market. Profit margins in these areas are very competitive with the rates of return being offered by the developing countries. Where thrift or other institutions are under pressure from capital inadequacies or other failings, they will be replaced by other domestic institutions to meet American credit demands.

In Europe within a few years, economic and financial integration will accelerate. Extraordinary opportunities will exist for financial institutions to consolidate, to increase their lending, and to increase their investing in a safe and more profitable market, much more so than has been true at any time in the entire postwar period.

In the Far East the opportunities are extraordinary. It is still possible to leverage portfolios and debt much more there than in the Latin American countries, where the leverage is already extremely high.

I believe these trends point to one major policy conclusion: the official side will have to do more, and the private side will have to be dragged along to accommodate the situation because its opportunities are more attractive elsewhere. From that viewpoint, the steps and measures announced by Mr. Brady today are helpful, but in the end it will be necessary to find ways to disguise one development that will have to be confronted in dealing with the Latin American debt and third world debt in general. The cost of that burden will have to be socialized, just as it has become necessary in the United States to socialize the cost of the savings and loan problems.

James D. Robinson III

I believe we are at last gaining momentum in the attack on the debt problem. Secretary Brady's initiative today represents a large advance toward realism in our appreciation of the nature of that problem.

In the next few days we will encounter statements to the effect that the Brady plan means the death of the Baker plan. My advice is to ignore those statements. The focus of both plans is on growth in the debtor countries. The principles of the Baker plan have not been abandoned. They will have to be embodied in the Brady plan as it is carried forward.

What is new, of course, is the explicit recognition of debt reduction as an essential element in the search for solutions. We have had a number of proposals that have included the concept of debt or debt service reduction. Charles Sanford of Bankers Trust has suggested a credit insurance facility, financed by creditor bank premium payments, to insure reduced interest payments on restructured debt. Ideas have come from other members of the financial fraternity, from members of Congress, and from economists in the academic world. I cannot resist putting in a plug for something I put forward a year ago called the International Institute of Debt and Development, or I2D2. It still is the most comprehensive of all the submissions on the table. The Brady statement is to some extent a collage of all these proposals. It is special in that it represents the official view of the American government.

Where do we go from here? I think that we should first welcome the news that the Treasury is reaching out to establish a dialogue with Japan about its role. Senator Sarbanes has properly emphasized the gap between our security expenditures and those of Japan, as well as the magnitude of Japan's external surplus. The Japanese, it seems clear, have been seeking a more active part in the debt drama, as witness the Miyazawa plan that was perhaps too hastily rejected last year. In any case, we must now look for Japan to provide, so to speak, some money in the wallet to go along with the will to act.

Next, I remain of the view that we are going to need an international facility to bring together all the players—the multilateral institutions, the debtors, the creditor banks, the industrial country governments—to manage the process. Such a facility was a central feature of I2D2. It could be attached to the IMF or to the World Bank or it could be a joint venture of the two institutions. Its locus can be argued, but the need for it, I think, will eventually have to be recognized. The Brady initiative, impressive as it is, does not tell us where the central leadership is to come from—leadership that will change the seemingly endless game of creditor bank-debtor country negotiations and provide an orderly procedure in which all the relevant parties are brought together to work out solutions. To repeat, we must manage the process.

Further, no one should suppose that debt reduction is a magic elixir. New money will be needed. Debt-equity swaps have a role. Structural reform is critical. Any developing country that puts forward a comprehensive direct investment code and supplements it with a sound intellectual property transfer code will find itself in the lead in the competition for foreign investment. The fact is that only with a credible environment for foreign investment will it be possible to get on a solid path to growth. With such an environment, moreover, flight capital will begin to return and make its contribution, which is potentially enormous, to a solution to the debt problem.

In Africa there are debtor nations in relation to which it has become respectable to use the X-rated term debt forgiveness. Even among these countries, some of them the poorest of the poor, there is a new-found appreciation for market-oriented reforms—not because of American sermonizing but because of evidence that market-oriented economies are the clear winners, as even the Soviet Union now recognizes.

To return to my beginning remarks. The secretary of the treasury has opened the way to a new and promising phase in our approach to third world debt. Now it will be necessary to rally the Group of Seven nations, chiefly Japan of course but the others as well. Thereafter we will have the economic summit where heads of government will have to convey the sense of urgency and the depth of commitment that the situation deserves. They should help us understand that the problem is not simply one that engages some of the banks in our several nations. It is a problem that involves economic well-being, trade balances, the fate of democratic institutions, and in the end our mutual security. Our leaders need to tell us all: get on with the job!

Seigo Nozaki

Although I am from the private financial sector, the Japanese Embassy has asked me to convey to this meeting a message from the minister of finance, Mr. Murayama, written after his learning of Secretary Brady's statement today.

"I would like to warmly welcome the announcement by U.S. Treasury Secretary Brady of a major strengthening of the strategy to deal with international debt problems. I strongly support the U.S. proposals, including voluntary market-based debt and debt service reduction and repatriation of flight capital.

"We have consulted closely with the U.S. financial authorities, and the U.S. proposals reflect an input based on the approach included in the Japanese proposal. We will work closely with the United States and other countries toward successful implementation of the strategy. In this connection, we intend to support the proposal financially, such as by increasing and strengthening parallel lending by the Export-Import Bank of Japan to the debtor countries, and by taking advantage of the strengthened debt strategy that includes provisions for debt reduction and debt service reduction."

My further comments of course are my own and do not necessarily represent either the views of the Japanese government or those of the institution where I now work.

Just before leaving Tokyo, I attended a conference where we had an in-depth discussion about the recycling of Japan's external surplus. As you know, the government has had a three-year program for recycling up to $30 billion. According to the data provided to our conference, almost 90 percent of the original plan has been completed. It is therefore incumbent on the government to consider new recycling measures. So Secretary Brady's remarks, including his reference to Japan's part in a somewhat new approach to third world debt, come at an appropriate time.

You will have noticed in Minister Murayama's message a mention of the prospective role of the Export-Import Bank of Japan in debt strategy. There is pending in the Diet amending legislation that would broaden the Export-Import Bank's powers. The preamble to the amendments cites Japan's enlarged role in the international economy, particularly referring to the debt problem, as requiring that the Bank be enabled to supplement and encourage commercial financing abroad.

The new authorities to be given to the Export-Import Bank of Japan are threefold.

First, the Bank will be permitted to take equity positions in private investments made abroad. This new authority is intended both to increase flows of capital to developing countries and to strengthen their private business sectors.

Second, the number of borrowers eligible for untied Bank loans is to be widened. Until now, only governmental institutions or enterprises were eligible for such loans. With this amendment, the Bank will be able to make untied loans to privatized public corporations and to public-private joint business entities. This provision will make it possible for the Bank to contribute more effectively to economic reform and restructuring programs.

Third, the Bank's guarantee powers will be enhanced. Corporations in which the Bank has equity shares will be eligible to receive guarantees for their long-term borrowings in proportion to the Bank's equity shares.

With these additional authorities lodged in its Export-Import Bank, the Japanese government will have significantly increased its flexibility in working for a resolution of the debt issue.

Let me offer, briefly, some views about the debt situation.

There can be no doubt that progress to date has been unsatisfactory. The volume of debt outstanding has grown beyond a trillion dollars, as we all know. Debt-to-export ratios have risen beyond 20 percent, and in some heavily indebted countries the ratios exceed 50 percent. Net capital flows to the third world are negative, a problem that is masked only by annual rescheduling on a very large scale.

Just a year ago former finance minister Miyazawa proposed a plan that had much in common with Secretary Brady's ideas as expressed today. Under the Miyazawa plan a debtor country, once it had agreed with the IMF on structural adjustment, would develop with its creditor banks a program to securitize a part of its debt at face value. The remaining debt would be rescheduled, under appropriate conditions. The debtor country would establish reserve accounts for the securitized and nonsecuritized portions of the debt, to be held in trust by the IMF. Thereafter the international financial institutions in the industrial countries would be expected to step up the flows of funds in support of structural adjustment.

From the point of view of the Japanese banks, the Miyazawa plan would have moved things in the right direction. I believe they will see the Brady plan in a similar light. Where they might well have misgivings would be in relation to debt reduction or write-offs of debt. Bank managers, with responsibilities to shareholders, will have difficulty with this concept. They would find it considerably easier to participate in interest rate reduction backed by some form of guarantee.

I will close these brief remarks with an old Japanese story about burden sharing, a subject that is of great current interest.

About a hundred years ago, so it is told, two honest men lived in the same small village. One was a plasterer named Kintaro, the other a carpenter, Kichigoro. One day while out walking, Kintaro found a silk wallet on the ground containing three gold coins, let us say $3.00. Together with the wallet was a seal, which told Kintaro that the wallet belonged to Kichigoro.

Being a man of impeccable honesty, Kintaro hastened to return the wallet to Kichigoro. But this equally honest carpenter refused to accept it. "I lost it. It is not mine any longer," he said. The two argued, to no conclusion. Finally their landlords—this was in feudal times, remember—brought them before Lord Oka, a magistrate famous not only for his fairness but also for his wit.

Having heard both sides of the case, Lord Oka told the two artisans that he was impressed with the exceptional honesty shown by each. "For this," he said, "you should be commended. Now let me see. Here we have $3.00 which neither of you claims. I will add $1.00 from my own pocket to make it $4.00. I will divide that equally and give you each $2.00 as a reward for your honesty and as an example for others."

He continued: "Kintaro, you could have pocketed the $3.00 but in your honesty you returned it. Receiving only $2.00, you have suffered a loss of $1.00. And you, Kichigoro, you had $3.00 before you lost your purse. Now you have $2.00 and you have lost $1.00. For myself I am short $1.00 from my own pocket. So each of us has shared equally in the loss."

The relevance of this ancient folk tale is, I think, that resolution of the third world debt issue will entail losses that will have to be shared—shared among debtors, creditors, international institutions, and, most likely, taxpayers. In question is whether we can find the wise magistrate to give us a result in which all can agree that the shares have been equal or, perhaps more appropriate, equitable.

Horst Schulmann

I take Secretary Brady's statement to be an important departure in debt strategy, but there is still much to learn about how his plan will work and how large its quantitative effect will be.

In general, I take the new approach to represent a continued evolution, not a revolutionary change, in debt strategy. It calls for continued cooperation between lenders and borrowers, which is also important because experience has shown that confrontation is not likely to work. I also strongly endorse Barber Conable's warning, referred to as well in Secretary Brady's statement, that we should not cut the heart out of the Baker plan. Its main elements continue to be valid.

Parenthetically, permit me to make a sales pitch. The Institute of International Finance in early January this year issued a report on the debt problem entitled "The Way Forward for Middle Income Countries." I commend it to you.

On one point I may differ from several speakers, possibly including Secretary Brady. I believe the core of the problem in these countries is neither the debt overhang nor the international environment. The level of external indebtedness and such events as the drop in the oil prices after 1985 aggravated the situation, but the problem is essentially domestic, since in the final analysis it can only be resolved at home.

A few examples may serve to make my point. Two countries—South Korea and Taiwan—exported as much in 1988 as the Baker 15, indeed more than all of Latin America. Further, South Korea in 1985 was the fourth largest debtor country in the world; as late as August 1985 it concluded a standby agreement with the IMF. Since then, it has repaid the IMF, repaid the World Bank, repaid most of the commercial banks, and is now on the brink of becoming a creditor country. All this occurred in the span of just four years. I emphasize that much can happen in a relatively short time when the right incentives and policies are in place.

I was pleased by the emphasis given today on capital flight. Silva Herzog said that six months ago nobody spoke about debt reduction. I would add that for the past few years there has not been enough talk about capital flight and the debtor countries' stock of external capital. To discuss the net worth of an ongoing concern without reference to all its assets is misleading, yet that is exactly what happens if the stock of flight capital from these countries is disregarded.

In any case, capital flight is not only an economic problem but also a political and a social problem, both in the debtor and creditor countries. In the creditor countries it is a political problem in that it is difficult to muster support for countries whose residents do not themselves have confidence in their government, as expressed by their continuing to send their capital abroad. In the debtor countries it is a serious political and social problem because only a very small minority of the people have exported wealth abroad. How, then, can the mass of the people be asked to make sacrifices if the capital flight problem is not under control?

The essential task in these countries is to restore market access and creditworthiness, which is tantamount to restoring the confidence of both domestic and foreign investors. The confidence of domestic investors will not be restored until flight capital returns on a large scale. Without the restoration of such confidence, these countries will find it difficult to compete internationally or to meet the aspirations of their people for economic growth and more satisfactory living standards.

As for debt reduction, I believe any mandatory form would choke off private capital flows for a long time to come. Thus the emphasis must be on the voluntary reduction of debt and debt servicing. It should be recognized that a substantial volume of voluntary debt and debt service reduction has taken place in the past few years, something on the order of $27 billion for the Baker 15 countries. The bulk of these market-based debt reduction transactions took place without any support from third parties, much of it in the form of debt-for-equity swaps and local currency conversions.

Debt for equity will continue to be important because of the direct link it provides to investment and growth. In this connection countries should be encouraged to open up their economies to foreign direct investment and to reform their investment codes.

Today new emphasis is accorded to voluntary debt reduction in the form of debt-for-debt exchanges. That is an area in which credit enhancements can make a difference, enhancements provided either by the debtor countries themselves or by third parties. I am grateful for the clarification by Secretary Brady that these programs would be negotiated between the debtor countries and their commercial bank creditors.

More generally, what commercial banks need in order to stay in the game is a wider menu of options and financial incentives. That applies to new money commitments as well as to voluntary debt reduction. Both must be made more attractive. One possibility is to improve opportunities for commercial bank cofinancing with the World Bank. There is an evident trade-off, a tension, between new money commitments and voluntary debt reduction. That trade-off can be addressed only on a country-by-country basis, which will mean a greater differentiation than before among Latin American countries in terms of their performance.

In sum, the time has come for more financial involvement on the official side, by the governments of the major creditor countries and the international financial institutions. The debt problem is simply too important to be left to the commercial banks and the debtor countries alone. In my view the Bush administration is calling for this greater involvement. By taking the leadership, the United States will provide opportunities for other countries to support and to expand on these ideas. In the end, however, the proof of the pudding is in the eating. We will have to see how big it is and how it will taste.

Bruce K. MacLaury

By way of summary, MacLaury made several points.

First, Bill Rogers's statement of the situation in Latin America could not help but impress everyone. He used the word desperation to characterize a continent.

Second, the statements and discussion have clearly legitimized the concepts of debt reduction and debt service reduction. This legitimacy came from the remarks of government officials, most notably Secretary Brady, from the heads of the international financial institutions, and from the commercial bankers themselves.

Third, a tension exists between characterizing the situation as desperate and saying at the same time that debt service or debt reduction could make only a modest contribution to an orderly solution of the third world debt problem.

Fourth, another kind of tension exists between finding ways of reducing debt and debt servicing and still maintaining the flow of new money. Minister Silva Herzog said he was optimistic that these two seemingly opposing forces could be reconciled, but he did not expand on this. While the task is by no means impossible, it will certainly be difficult.

Fifth, a clear consensus emerged that the next phase of debt strategy must build on the Baker plan. There is no substitute for new money, just as there is no substitute for structural adjustment and policy reform in the developing countries.

Finally, some other features were attached to this new phase in debt strategy. Henry Kaufman characterized third world debt as being no longer solely a bank problem or a developing country problem, but a problem for the international system. Ways would have to be found to socialize it. Jim Robinson saw Secretary Brady's initiative as a beginning foray leading to widening discussion of the issue in subsequent meetings of the Group of 7 and in economic summits. In any event, a new sense of official leadership is in evidence, which may in the future be seen as a threshold in the management of a difficult, major world problem.

Conference Participants

with their affiliations at the time of the conference

Philippe Adhemar
French Embassy

Francisco J. Aguirre-Sacasa
World Bank

Nobutoshi Akao
Japanese Embassy

Nancy Alexander
Friends Committee on National Legislation

William Alexander
Institute of International Finance

James E. Ammerman
U.S. Department of the Treasury

John B. Anderson
Bretton Woods Committee

David Apgar
Office of Senator Bradley

Mauricio Garcia Araujo
Venezuelan Banco Centrale

Roy L. Ash
Ash Capital Corporation

Robert E. Asher
Bretton Woods Committee

Cesar Atala
Ambassador of Peru

Robert Baker
U.S. Department of the Treasury

Harvey Bale
Hewlett-Packard Corporation

Frank Ballance
James Orr Associates

Joseph W. Barr
Bretton Woods Committee

Andrew Bartels
American Express

Bernie Barth
Bank of Montreal

Steve Beckman
UAW–International Union

Robert Bench
Price Waterhouse

Robert Berg
International Development Conference

C. Fred Bergsten
Institute for International Economics

Willard M. Berry
National Foreign Trade Council

Christine A. Bindert
Shearson Lehman Hutton

Richard Bissell
Agency for International Development

Charles Blitzer
Massachusetts Institute of Technology

David Bock
World Bank

Gerhard Boehmer
World Bank

Roger Bolton
U.S. Department of the Treasury

Daniel Bond
Export-Import Bank

Pam Bradley
International Monetary Fund

Bill Bradley
U.S. Senate

Nicholas F. Brady
U.S. Department of the Treasury

Lawrence J. Brainard
Bankers Trust Company

Henry Breck
National Resource Defense Council

Robert Browne
House Banking Committee

Ralph C. Bryant
Brookings Institution

James B. Burnham
Mellon Bank

Robert Burns
James Orr Associates

Nan Burroughs
Inter-American Development Bank

Jacques Bussiers
Bank of Canada

Louis W. Cabot
Cabot Corporation

Michel Camdessus
International Monetary Fund

Wallace J. Campbell
CARE International

Don Carlson
Office of Congressman Kennedy

Jack Carlson
Bretton Woods Committee

Frank Cassell
International Monetary Fund

Haydee Celaya
National Bank of Washington

Mary Chavez
U.S. Department of the Treasury

Terrence Checki
N.Y. Federal Reserve Bank

George J. Clark
Citicorp

A. W. Clausen
BankAmerica Corporation

Edwin Clock
Comptroller of the Currency

William T. Coleman, Jr.
O'Melveny & Myers

Barber Conable
World Bank

Mark Constantine
House Banking Committee

Gala Cooke
National Association of Negro Women

John Costello
Citizens Network

Margaret Coullard
American Soybean Association

Lloyd N. Cutler
Wilmer, Cutler & Pickering

William B. Dale
Bretton Woods Committee

Elizabeth Dalton
U.S. Department of the Treasury

Jonathan Davidson
University of South Carolina

Peter J. Davies
Interaction

Richard Debs
Morgan Stanley International

Robert Devlin
UN Economic Commission
for Latin America

Rimmer deVries
Morgan Guaranty Trust

C. Douglas Dillon
Bretton Woods Committee

Job Dittberner
Atlantic Council

Steve Dizard
Salomon Brothers

John Donaldson
Black, Manafort, Stone & Kelly

Nick Donatiello
Office of Senator Bradley

Robert F. Drinan, S.J.
Georgetown University Law Center

Philip A. DuSault
Office of Management and Budget

Stephen Ecton
U.S. Department of State

Takashi Eguchi
Japan Center
for International Finance

Stuart E. Eizenstat
Powell, Goldstein, Frazer & Murphy

Richard D. Erb
International Monetary Fund

John H. Falb
NCNB, Texas

Thomas L. Farmer
Bankers for Foreign Trade

Walter Fauntroy
U.S. House of Representatives

Richard E. Feinberg
Overseas Development Council

Martin Feldstein
National Bureau of Economic Research

R. W. Fischer
Soypro International

Dennis Flannery
World Bank

Henry H. Fowler
Former Secretary of the Treasury

Isaiah Frank
School for Advanced International
Studies

Harry Freeman
American Express

Orville L. Freeman
Popham, Haik

Jerome Fried
Economic Consultant

Edward R. Fried
Brookings Institution

Henry H. Frothingham
Bank of Boston

Richard Gardner
Columbia University

Jean Paul Gimon
Crédit Lyonnais

Ronnie Goldberg
U.S. Council for International Business

Aaron Goldman
Salomon Brothers

Katherine Graham
Washington Post Company

Carol Grigsby
Agency for International Development

Guenther Grosche
International Monetary Fund

Martin J. Gruenberg
*U.S. Senate Banking, Housing
and Urban Affairs Committee*

Kenneth A. Guenther
Independent Bankers

Marino Gurfinkel
Petroleos de Venezuela S.A.

Xavier Gurza
Mexican Embassy

Barry Hager
*Office of Congressman
Bruce Morrison*

Joseph W. Harned
Atlantic Council

John M. Harrington
U.S. Department of State

Helmut Hartman
International Monetary Fund

John Haseltine
Institute of International Finance

F. William Hawley
Citicorp

Margaret Daly Hayes
Inter-American Development Bank

Caroline Haynes
U.S. Department of the Treasury

Dan Heininger
Coudert Brothers

William Hellert
Overseas Development Council

William A. Hewitt
Bretton Woods Committee

Roderick M. Hills
Manchester Group

Donald P. Hilty
Chrysler Corporation

Luther H. Hodges, Jr.
National Bank of Washington

Daniel Hofgren
Goldman Sachs

Christian R. Holmes IV
*Former administrator of Trade and
Development Program*

Steven A. Hopkins
Citicorp

W. David Hopper
World Bank

Thomas L. Hughes
*Carnegie Endowment
for International Peace*

Arthur W. Hummel, Jr.
Former U.S. Ambassador to China

Enrique V. Iglesias
Inter-American Development Bank

Mr. Ishihara
Bank of Tokyo

Shafiqul Islam
Council on Foreign Relations

Tadashi Iwashita
Japanese Embassy

Stephanie James
Bretton Woods Committee

U. Alexis Johnson
Atlantic Council

Peter T. Jones
University of California, Berkeley

Jill Judy
Bretton Woods Committee

Helen B. Junz
International Monetary Fund

Yoshiaki Kaneko
Japanese Embassy

Yusuke Kashiwagi
Bank of Tokyo

Samuel Katz
Georgetown University

Henry Kaufman
Henry Kaufman and Company

Tadashi Kawabe
Japan Center for International Finance

Robert B. Keating
World Bank

Christopher Kennan
Rockefeller Foundation

Colbert I. King
Riggs National Bank

David Kline
Hillsboro Associates

Wolfgang W. Koenig
Bank of N.Y./Irving Trust

Sachio Kohjima
Bank of Tokyo

James L. Kohnen
NMS

Jurgen Koppen
European Commission

Charles Kovacs
Chase Manhattan Bank

Michael Krakowski
HWWA

Timothy Krause
U.S. Department of the Treasury

K. Krowacki
International Monetary Fund

Faye Ku
Bretton Woods Committee

Pedro-Pablo Kuczynski
First Boston International

Thomas Layman
Institute of International Finance

Jim Leach
U.S. House of Representatives

Marc E. Leland
Marc E. Leland & Associates

Wilbert J. LeMelle
Mercy College

William E. Leonhard
Parsons Corporation

Howard Lewis
National Association of Manufacturers

Ronald A. Lindhart
Comptroller of the Currency

Sol M. Linowitz
Coudert Brothers

Karen Lisaker
Columbia University

Gabriel Locher
Manufacturers National Bank of Detroit

Nora Lustig
Brookings Institution

Eugene McAllister
U.S. Department of State

Paul M. McGonagle
First Chicago Corporation

James T. McIntyre, Jr.
McNair Law Firm

Bruce K. MacLaury
Brookings Institution

R. T. McNamar
Conover & McNamar

Salvador Madrigal
Latin Merchant Bank

Bruce R. Magid
Bank of America

Judith Maguire
World Bank

Eugene Marans
Cleary, Gottlieb, Steen & Hamilton

Fred J. Martin
Bank of America

Sandra Masur
Eastman Kodak Company

Charles McC. Mathias, Jr.
Jones, Day, Reavis & Pogue

Lawrence Mellinger
Inter-American Development Bank

William B. Milam
U.S. Department of State

Azizali Mohammed
International Monetary Fund

Nancy Morrison
Bretton Woods Committee

Robert Myers
World Bank

Arnold Nachmanoff
Oxford Analytica

Walter Neuhaus
Deutschebanke

Nancy Newman
League of Women Voters

Mary Noblit
Bretton Woods Committee

Seigo Nozaki
Sumitomo Life Insurance

Katherine O'Neill
International Monetary Fund

Fernando Oaxaca
Coronado Communications

Charlotte Orr
James Orr Associates

James C. Orr
Bretton Woods Committee

Robert D. Orr
Former Governor, Indiana

Joe Ortega
Maryland National Bank

Henry Owen
Consultants International Group

J. William Peterson
Construction Industry Manufacturers Association

Carlos E. Paredes
Brookings Institution

Douglas A. Paul
American International Group

Rudolph A. Peterson
Former chairman, Bank of America

John Petty
Former chairman, Marine Midland

J. B. L. Pierce
Boeing Company

Georges Pineau
International Monetary Fund

Jorge Pinto
World Bank

Godert Posthumous
International Monetary Fund

Ernest Preeg
Center for Strategic and International Studies

Ronald E. Pump
AT&T

Steve Quick
Joint Economic Committee

Holly Rafkin-Sax
Manufacturers Hanover

Thomas F. Railsback
Nash, Railsback & Plesso

Myer Rashish
Rashish Associates

Frank Record
Export-Import Bank

Alfred Reifman
Congressional Research Service

Jacques J. Reinstein
Atlantic Council

Nicholas Rey
Bear Stearns & Company

S. Melvin Rines
Kidder Peabody

Charles W. Robinson
Energy Transition Corporation

James D. Robinson III
American Express

David Rockefeller
Former chairman, Chase Manhattan

William D. Rogers
Arnold & Porter

H. Chapman Rose
Brookings Institution

John Ross
Debt for Development Coalition

Don Roth
World Bank

Bill Ryan
Kidder Peabody

Francisco Saenz
Saenz Projects

Thibault de Saint Phalle
Saint Phalle International Group

Paul S. Sarbanes
U.S. Senate

Horst Schulmann
Institute of International Finance

Elizabeth Schwartz
Boeing Company

William Seidman
Federal Deposit Insurance Corporation

John Williamson Sewell
Overseas Development Council

Alexander Shakow
World Bank

John Shilling
World Bank

L. Parks Shipley
Bank of N.Y./Irving Trust

Jesús Silva Herzog
Former Mexican Minister of Finance

John J. Simone
Manufacturers Hanover Trust

Karna Small
Hill & Knowlton

Tim Smith
Federal Reserve

Robert Solomon
Brookings Institution

Komal S. Sri-Kumar
Drexel Burnham

J. William Stanton
World Bank

Ray Sternfield
Inter-American Development Bank

Elizabeth Stewart
U.S. Department of the Treasury

Abby Sutherland
Bretton Woods Committee

Morris Tanenbaum
AT&T Communications

S. A. Taubenblatt
Bechtel Group

Nelle Temple
House Banking Committee

Donald Terry
House Committee on Small Business

Dietmar Thorand
Embassy of the Federal Republic of Germany

Philip H. Trezise
Brookings Institution

Raymond Vernon
Kennedy School of Government

Frank Vogl
World Bank

Paul A. Volcker
James D. Wolfensohn Inc.

Frank Vukmanic
U.S. Department of the Treasury

Rodney B. Wagner
Morgan Guaranty Trust

Charls E. Walker
Charls Walker Associates

C. Maxwell Watson
International Monetary Fund

Murray L. Weidenbaum
Center for Strategic and International Studies

Jonathan R. Weinstein
Bretton Woods Committee

Larry Williams
Sierra Club

Derish M. Wolff
Louis Berger International

Rob Wright
World Bank Watch

Koji Yamasaki
International Monetary Fund